NEGOTI...

SKILL...S...

Alan Fowler's career spans the private and public sectors, with personnel appointments in four industries (engineering, shoe manufacture, sugar, and construction) and two large local authorities (the Greater London Council and Hampshire County Council). He is now a freelance personnel consultant, a director of Personnel Publications Ltd (publishers of the IPD's fortnightly magazine, *People Management*), and a member of the editorial advisory board of that magazine.

In his personnel appointments he had extensive experience of negotiating with many trade unions at workplace, company, and national level, including a period as head of the GLC's industrial relations division. Some of his recent consultancy assignments have also included advice to private- and public-sector clients on the handling of complex negotiations related to organisational restructuring and the redesign of remuneration systems.

He writes widely on personnel and management topics, with frequent articles in *People Management* and a monthly column in the management weekly, *Local Government Chronicle*. His books published by the IPD include *Employee Induction: A good start* (3rd edn, 1996), *Get More – and More Results – from Your People* (1998), *Get More – and More Value – from Your People* (1998), and two titles in the IPD's Management Shapers series, *Negotiating, Persuading and Influencing* and *The Disciplinary Interview*.

The Institute of Personnel and Development is the leading publisher of books and reports for personnel and training professionals, students, and all those concerned with the effective management and development of people at work. For details of all our titles, please contact the Publishing Department:

tel. 0181-263 3387

fax 0181-263 3850

e-mail publish@ipd.co.uk

The catalogue of all IPD titles can be viewed on the IPD website:

http://www.ipd.co.uk

NEGOTIATION SKILLS AND STRATEGIES

Second Edition

Alan Fowler

INSTITUTE OF PERSONNEL AND DEVELOPMENT

First published 1990
Reprinted 1992, 1994
Second edition 1996
Reprinted 1999

Phototypeset by Fakenham Photosetting Ltd, Fakenham, Norfolk
and printed in Great Britain by Short Run Press, Exeter

British Library Cataloguing-in-Publication Data
A catalogue record for this book is available from the
British Library.

ISBN 0-85292-664-2

**INSTITUTE OF PERSONNEL
AND DEVELOPMENT**

IPD House, Camp Road, London SW19 4UX
Tel: 0181 971 9000   Fax: 0181 263 3333
Registered office as above. Registered Charity No. 1038333
A company limited by guarantee. Registered in England No. 2931892

Contents

Preface

The ability to influence and persuade is one of the most essential of all management skills – and influence and persuasion are very much the stuff of effective negotiation. These skills are particularly important for the personnel professional who, in an advisory and internal consultancy role, is rarely in a position to get results by direct executive action. Line managers often need to be convinced about the merits of personnel initiatives before they will commit themselves to action; concluding satisfactory collective agreements or negotiating contracts are also a matter of discussion and eventual joint agreement.

Within the personnel context, it might be thought that the primary negotiating activity is formal collective bargaining with trade unions. That was certainly the view during the 1970s, when the personnel role was strongly focused on industrial relations – often of a confrontational nature. Industrial conflict at that time also generated the stereotype of the tough, manipulative negotiator doing deals in smoke-filled corridors. But although this type of negotiation is now far less common, collective bargaining is still an important function, and in the late 1990s there are indications of a resurgence in trade union activity after the relatively quiescent industrial relations scene of the previous decade. However, it would be taking too narrow a view of negotiation to limit the subject to this one specialised aspect. It would also be dangerous to assume that the confrontational style of traditional industrial relations negotiation provides an effective model – even for collective bargaining, let alone for the broader and often more informal processes described in this book.

The book has been written with personnel professionals in mind, although most of the skills and strategies involved are also relevant to managers at large. Most managers, whether in specialist roles or in the line, spend a large proportion of their time in contact with other managers over whom they have no executive authority. Situations frequently occur in which two or more managers need to reach agreement in order to make progress, and the process of exploring initial differences of view and reaching an agreed conclusion is essentially one of negotiation, whether or not the participants recognise it as such. With the growth of organisational concepts such as the internal market and in-house consultancy, many managers are also being placed in purchaser and provider roles, requiring a more systematic and quasi-commercial approach to the definition of what the internal customer needs and how best the in-house supplier can meet these needs. Outsourcing, market-testing, and competitive tendering have also widened the range of commercial transactions that managers, including personnel professionals, have to handle. All these activities involve negotiation, and their skilful management has a direct impact on organisational performance. The skilful negotiator adds value to the business – an important factor for personnel professionals to demonstrate if they are to achieve the recognition and status that an effective personnel function merits.

The book is essentially practical in style and includes many short case-studies to illustrate the principles discussed. These case-studies are not restricted to personnel examples, partly because the principles apply to managers in all disciplines, and partly because personnel and development professions may find it useful to draw on these cases as material for training courses in negotiation for managers at large. Those requiring more detailed training material will find this in the booklet *Negotiating, Persuading and Influencing* in the IPD's Training Extras series.

The text of this book is based on that of the first edition, *Negotiation: Skills and strategies* (IPM 1990), which in turn was developed from my original book on the subject, *Effective Negotiation* (IPM 1986). Both these books are now out of print. Their underlying theme – and that of the current text – is that negotiation should be seen as a constructive process contributing to organisational success, not as a battle for the preservation of personal or corporate power or prestige.

1

Understanding Basic Principles

To many personnel managers, negotiation implies collective bargaining. To a sales executive, it will be thought of in terms of making a commercial deal. Quantity surveyors, purchasing managers and lawyers all have their own specialist interpretations of what, in essence, is a process common to all managerial work. For, in reality, all managers negotiate, if not with outside parties then with each other.

The procedures and language of formal negotiation vary with the type of negotiation involved. A set-piece pay bargaining session has its own system and jargon that differ from those of a meeting of solicitors to settle a claim for libel damages. Yet the underlying principles and much of the psychology of the process are the same for all forms of negotiation.

It is also easy for managers to overlook the fact that much of their informal daily activity is, in effect, negotiation. All managers spend a large proportion of their time trying to influence and persuade other managers over whom they have no executive authority. Consider two examples:

A personnel manager attempts to 'sell' the need for a more systematic form of employee consultation to a reluctant office manager. The company has a general policy of support for employee involvement practices, but has not laid down any specific system or procedure. Neither the extent to which the personnel manager can use the general policy to require the office manager's co-operation, nor the right of the office manager to reject the personnel manager's suggestions is clearly defined. The outcome will be influenced by their possibly differing perceptions of the formal position, and by the powers of argument or persuasion of the personnel manager.

A sales executive tries to persuade the production manager to

1

change a manufacturing schedule to fit in a small order for a special customer. The production manager has full authority to decide production schedules against a weekly output plan set by top management. Officially, the sales manager should make a request through the sales director for an urgent variation to this plan but, because the order is only a small one, he approaches the production manager informally and must, therefore, rely on persuasion.

Negotiating skills are, therefore, a very important element in the effective manager's portfolio of personal competencies. They are included as such in the set of managerial competencies required to achieve a management qualification at Level 5 of the National Vocational Qualification system.

A definition

Recognising when negotiation is occurring is the first step towards acquiring the necessary skills, and this is aided by an understanding of the basic principles involved.

Negotiation is a process, not a single skill. A range of skills are involved in handling this process effectively, but to identify the skills relevant to any negotiating episode, it is important to recognise which elements or principles of negotiation are involved. There are seven principles common to all forms of negotiation:

- Negotiation involves two or more parties who need – or think they need – each other's involvement in achieving some desired outcome. There must be some common interest, either in the subject matter of the negotiation or in the negotiating context, that puts or keeps the parties in contact.
- Although sharing a degree of interest, the parties start with different opinions or objectives, and these differences initially prevent the achievement of an outcome.
- At least initially, the parties consider that negotiation is a more satisfactory way of trying to resolve their differences than alternatives such as coercion or arbitration.
- Each party considers that there is some possibility of persuading the other to modify their original position. It is not essential – though it is usually highly desirable – for each party to be

2

willing to compromise. But negotiation can begin when parties have an initial intention of maintaining their opening positions: but each has some hope of persuading the other to change.

● Similarly, even when their ideal outcomes prove unattainable, both parties retain hope of an acceptable final agreement.

● Each party has some influence or power – real or assumed – over the other's ability to act. If one party is entirely powerless, there may be no point in the other party committing itself to a negotiating process. The matter can be settled unilaterally by the party with the untrammelled power to act. This power or influence may, however, be indirect and bear on issues other than those that are the direct subject of negotiation.

● The negotiating process itself is one of interaction between people – in most cases by direct, verbal interchange. Even when the negotiation is being conducted through correspondence, there is an essential underlying human element. The progress of all types of negotiation is strongly influenced by emotion and attitudes, not just by the facts or logic of each party's arguments.

Putting all these principles together, a definition emerges that provides a summary and a starting-point for a detailed examination of the various parts of the process, and the strategies and skills involved.

> Negotiation is a process of interaction by which two or more parties who consider they need to be jointly involved in an outcome, but who initially have different objectives, seek by the use of argument and persuasion to resolve their differences in order to achieve a mutually acceptable solution.

It will probably be readily accepted that this definition is relevant to formal negotiations such as pay bargaining or the settlement of a legal claim for damages. Trade unions and employers – or the solicitors representing two parties to litigation – obviously accept that they need jointly to evolve a mutually satisfactory outcome, starting from differing positions. Each party knows that the other has some power to influence the outcome. A trade union might apply the sanction of industrial action: an employer might reduce the labour force: the claimant's solicitors might stop negotiating and take the case to court: the respondent has some defence if this occurs. But how does the definition apply to the examples given earlier of managers trying to persuade their colleagues to accept new courses of action? In the second of these examples, the sales executive has no direct power to require the production manager to alter production schedules: the production manager can just say no – so where does negotiation come in? A willingness at least to consider the request – and thereby become involved in a discussion about a possible jointly satisfactory outcome – will stem from several aspects of common interest, or from a recognition of more subtle forms of power.

The sales executive wants the production schedules altered, the production manager does not, but both managers, it is to be hoped, share an interest in the success of the business. To disappoint an important customer may be of more immediate concern to the sales executive than to the production manager, but a good production manager will pay heed to the importance of good customer service. Similarly, the sales executive will recognise the costs and perhaps delays to other orders that a change in the production schedule might give rise to. So a common interest in the good of the business enables both to see something in the other's point of view, and thus encourages a dialogue, rather than the simple exercise of formal authority.

It may be that the sales executive (or the customer on whose behalf the request is being made) is known by the production manager to be highly regarded by the managing director. It might thus be unwise, in terms of company politics, for the production manager to run the risk of being considered unhelpful.

Both managers also know that they have to continue to work together. Without anything being said, both will probably be influenced by knowing that this long-term working relationship could be adversely affected by mishandling the particular incident. The production manager may have the right to say no – in other words, not to negotiate – but will wonder whether this would cause avoidable friction. There may also be the thought that by agreeing some concession, an obligation may be created that might be capitalised on at some future date.

4

In the other example, considerations of a similar kind might also lead to the office manager's being willing to discuss the personnel manager's advice. Both have an interest in the smooth running of the company and in compliance with the company policy: the personnel manager may be known to have top management backing; the managers have to go on working together, and therefore the office manager will have to consider the implications of rejecting the personnel manager's advice if employee relations are then seen to deteriorate.

Negotiation and consultation

These examples illustrate situations in which, despite an uneven distribution of power, each party accepts either that the other has some right to influence the outcome, or that a jointly evolved solution is more desirable than an imposed one. It is not unusual, however, for managers to find themselves unexpectedly in a negotiating situation – often because they confuse consultation with negotiation. Consider this example:

Jane Tonbridge is the newly appointed finance manager of a bus company. She decides to reorganise her department and is told by the chief executive that she has *carte blanche* to do so, provided she avoids additional expenditure. He suggests, though, that she might care to have a chat with Bill Truscott, the long-serving operations manager. She draws up her plans for restructuring her department, sees Bill, tells him the plans, outlines their advantages as she sees them, and finishes by saying, 'I hope you agree.' Whereupon Bill ponders for a moment and then says, 'Sorry, but I don't. You would do better to keep things as they are.'

Jane now has an awkward choice. She can say in effect, 'I'm sorry about that – but it's my department and I was only sounding you out, not asking for your approval.' Alternatively, she can begin to argue the pros and cons of her and Bill's ideas. If she does this, which is clearly more tactful if less satisfactory to her than rebuffing Bill, she has begun negotiating. Tacitly, she will be accepting a need to reach a conclusion that Bill accepts. This outcome may well lead to a very different reorganisation from the one she would ideally like.

What has gone wrong for Jane is that a process she intended as consultation has been interpreted by the other party as an invitation to negotiate because of the way she approached the discussion. To achieve a true consultative approach, she should have seen Bill before finalising her plans, saying something like, 'I'm looking at how my department operates: is there anything from your point of view that you think I should take into account?' This would leave her free to develop her own plans; it implies no commitment to accept any specific proposal by Bill; it does not place him in a position to express approval. It is genuine consultation. The difference from negotiation is crucial, and can be summarised in two further definitions:

Negotiation implies acceptance by both parties that agreement between them is required (or is desirable) before a decision can be implemented.

Consultation implies a willingness by one party to listen to the views of the other, while reserving the right to make a final decision, whether or not the other party is in agreement.

This distinction is sometimes difficult to sustain, particularly when, in a discussion that begins in a consultative mode, one party or the other raises an issue that necessitates joint agreement, thus switching the discussion to negotiation. One situation in which this may occur is during a consultative discussion about a potential redundancy. The employer may treat this as consultative on the basis that there is no question but that the job concerned will be disbanded. The employee may, however, unexpectedly suggest a transfer to a different job as an alternative to redundancy, provided certain conditions can be met regarding, say, an allowance for additional travelling time. If the employer is prepared to consider this suggestion, but is not immediately agreeable to the proposed travel payment, the matter becomes one of negotiation, which may lead to an eventual compromise satisfactory to both parties.

Recent employment legislation has compounded the possibility of confusion between consultation and negotiation by the revised provisions in the Trade Union Reform and Employment Rights Act 1993 relating to consultation about impending collective redundancies. The Act sets out a schedule of matters that must form the subject of what is defined as consultation with either the recognised trade unions or (in accordance with the later 1995 regulations) elected employee representatives. Prior to this Act, it was clear that what was required was consultation in accordance with the definition given above. Employers were expected to provide adequate information about the situation, listen to what the trade unions had to say, and respond to the unions' views – if necessary by explaining why these views could not be accepted. There was no implication that any form of agreement was needed: the employer clearly retained the sole right of decision. But the 1993 Act, in addition to expanding the range of subjects to be discussed, went on to state that consultation should be conducted 'with a view to reaching agreement'. This sounds like negotiation, and it is (understandably) being interpreted as such by trade unions in some redundancy situations.

However, although it is obviously desirable from the viewpoint of good employment practice to proceed with redundancies if possible on an agreed basis, the legal position remains that this form of employer/trade union discussion is consultative. The law and the courts expect employers to make a genuine effort to obtain trade unions' or employee representatives' agreement to the redundancy action proposed, but do not require actual agreement to be reached or the proposed action to be blocked if the effort fails. The employer's actual or implied message to the trade unions must be 'We shall go as far as we can in meeting the points you raise, but at the end of the day we retain the right to make the decisions we feel are necessary.'

Similar situations may occur in works councils, whether these are long-established joint consultative committees or the new kind, which an increasing number of multinational companies are setting up to meet EU requirements. The intention is that they should be genuinely joint employer/employee bodies in which differences between management and staff are put aside for the sake of the organisation as a whole. Both sides share the long-term goal of company survival and success, so the council's role is to emphasise this commonality of interest. Its activities should include two-way communication, discussion, and exploration of ideas from whatever source, and hopefully a degree of joint decision-making. Works councils are *not* intended to get involved in collective bargaining about pay and conditions of employment. This is, however, not how it always works out in practice. If managers are reluctant to share information about business issues with employee representatives, or if such representatives display a narrow concern with the effects of company plans on earnings and working practices, conflicting views are likely to develop into confrontational negotiation. Managers and staff may need help in adjusting to a new form of joint working, in which inevitable differences of opinion are seen as helpful in ensuring that all aspects of a topic are defined rather than as matters for dispute. Resolving such differences should be a positive process, building on common interests and points of agreement.

There is an element of negotiation in this type of discussion, but it is very different from situations in which each party tries to establish a winning position for itself. The strategy should be to test the validity of different viewpoints against the agreed objectives (or mission, or values) of the company. Distinguishing between short- and long-term interests and outcomes is often a key feature in the avoidance of unconstructive disputes; referring serious disagreements on matters such as pay to a separate negotiating body can also help maintain the wider role of an effective works council.

Is negotiation necessary?

One aspect of effective negotiation is therefore to decide or recognise in advance whether a particular interaction will require negotiation or whether it can be kept at consultation.

Negotiation can be a lengthy process and, by asking whether it is necessary, time may sometimes be saved and unnecessary compromise avoided. On occasions, a request to negotiate may best be met by pointing out that the party making the request has no standing in the matter. If a manager has the undoubted authority to act, making a decision rather than negotiating about it may be the best tactic.

Alternatively, there are cases in which the best response to a request or a claim is to concede it without argument. Why waste time negotiating if the other party has a good case and there are no adverse consequences in conceding? Unnecessary negotiation, followed, perhaps, by a grudging concession of the other party's claim, will lose all the advantage that might be gained with a quick unexpected yes.

An alternative to a simple yes or no when a difference of view occurs is to skip negotiation and proceed immediately to some form of third-party intervention. On the most formal basis, this might imply a decision to take a dispute to court: informally, two managers who quickly realise that they cannot reach agreement about a working problem may jointly agree to stop wasting time in argument and refer the matter to a senior manager for resolution.

A good general rule is: *do not* negotiate unless you have to – or unless you can obtain some direct or indirect advantage by doing so.

Stages in negotiation

Assuming negotiation *is* necessary or desirable, three stages need to be handled well:

- a preparation phase before the negotiation begins
- the actual negotiating process – the interaction that leads to an agreement about an outcome
- the implementation of the agreement (or agreement as to how the outcome is to be implemented) – a stage sometimes given too little attention because of a preoccupation with winning the negotiating arguments.

Preparation

Negotiations need to be planned; several later chapters deal in detail with such aspects as assessing the relative strength of the parties and the setting of negotiating objectives. Two preliminary questions are useful:

- What are the real issues?
- Which parties should be involved?

The first question is often of particular importance in industrial relations, as the following example illustrates:

> George Truscott was the regional personnel manager of an insurance company. The regional office had recently been reorganised, with several new young section managers brought in from other branches. Over a three-month period, the trade union representative of the premiums section brought a series of complaints to George about heating, lighting, the design of new office furniture, and the new office layout. This culminated in a formal demand by the union for a meeting to discuss and resolve all these housekeeping issues.
>
> George felt that other matters might lie behind this apparent general dissatisfaction with the physical aspects of the office, and that to attempt to negotiate just on these aspects might not improve matters. Instead of setting up a formal meeting, he therefore had a preliminary informal talk with the union representative. From this conversation it became evident that the real, though underlying, issue was resentment by the premiums staff about the imposition, as they saw it, of a young, brash, uncommunicative manager from another branch. This indicated that a different negotiating strategy would have to be evolved – even though some aspects of housekeeping did need to be addressed.

The question as to which parties should be involved sometimes occurs in an industrial relations context, and frequently needs consideration when informal managerial negotiations take place.

With trade unions, negotiations may occur with manual or production workers about changes in working practices. These changes may have an effect on the jobs of white-collar staff, and it has not been unknown for companies to conclude agreements with their manual trade unions before recognising that parallel negotiations are necessary to secure the co-operation of the clerical or other support staff. Inadequate attention had been paid to the question of who needs to be involved.

Similar problems can occur when two managers meet to discuss an issue that is also of concern to a third. Thus, a change to factory maintenance schedules, agreed between a chief engineer and a production manager, may have implications for the stores operation managed by the purchasing manager. Omitting the latter from the discussion will probably mean that his or her initial reaction to the change will be unhelpful.

During negotiation

The whole negotiating process is dealt with in detail in succeeding chapters. Here, it is enough to note that most effective negotiations follow a six-stage pattern:

- The parties start by agreeing what it is they are negotiating about – they define the issues.
- Each side then sets out what it is seeking, or the side making a claim puts its case, and the other party gives an initial response – they define their initial positions.
- There is then a more open phase when the initial positions are tested in argument.
- The parties then move to a tentative exploration of possible outcomes.
- Firm or formal proposals are then made, discussed, and perhaps modified.
- Finally, an agreement is defined and concluded.

Implementation

Ill-defined agreements, or agreements that have paid too little attention to the practicalities of implementation, frequently collapse soon after they have been concluded. Although the purpose of negotiation is to achieve an agreement, the purpose of an agreement must be to implement some positive action. Three steps can help to prevent an implementation failure:

- In all but the most informal of negotiations, confirm in writing what has been agreed.
- If appropriate, include an implementation programme in the agreement. In other words, agree who is committed to doing what by when – do not leave this undefined to become the subject of later disagreement.
- Ensure that everyone concerned is told about the agreement, what it implies, and the action that will follow. In many cases, the need for this information will be much wider than just the persons who took part in the actual negotiations.

11

Key points

● All managers negotiate – with each other, as well as with customers, suppliers, trade unions, and other outside parties.

● Negotiation is about achieving a mutually acceptable outcome to a situation in which the parties involved initially have differing aims.

● Negotiations are affected by the emotions and attitudes of the negotiators – not just by the logic of the arguments they use.

● Consultation needs to be distinguished from negotiation. In negotiation, the parties accept that joint agreement is necessary; in consultation, one party reserves the right to act unilaterally.

● Do not negotiate unless either this is necessary or some advantage may be obtained by so doing.

● Three stages are involved: preparation, the negotiation itself, and implementation.

2

Weighing Relative Strengths

Before embarking on negotiation, it is important to assess the strength of each side's bargaining position. In an informal managerial situation, factors such as the extent to which a manager's proposals are backed by company policy or by the availability of resources affect the assessment. Being in a strong bargaining position implies that one party has more power than the other to influence the outcome in the direction one prefers. In an industrial relations context, assessing the other side may mean considering whether, by taking industrial action, the trade union could prevent the implementation of the employer's proposals. On the union side, an assessment may be made of the likelihood of the employer's obtaining an injunction to prevent industrial action. The exercise of this power is often more indirect than industrial or legal action. Negatively, it may consist of generating inconvenience through delays – a not uncommon feature of legal negotiations – or of creating an unpleasant or irritating working relationship. In a positive sense, it implies that one party can offer more advantage or benefit in support of its case than the other. It is rare for an assessment of relative strength to be capable of precise calculation, or to be reduced to a simple arithmetical calculation. It is normally a matter of judgement, in which at least four forms of power or influence are involved:

- the degree of authority or ability that each party possesses to make and implement decisions about the matter in question
- the ability of each party to influence the other through some form of sanction or benefit; which may be unrelated to the matter under negotiation
- the strength of the arguments in favour of each party's case in terms of logic or equity
- the determination with which each party pursues its case.

Two examples can be used to illustrate how assessments of each of these aspects may influence negotiating strategy:

Jill Wright is the advertising sales manager for a computer journal. Her job is to maximise income from the sale of advertising space to computer and software suppliers. She knows she could sell more space if the journal ran major articles, planned several months in advance, on topics suggested by advertisers and to which their advertisements could be related.
Gordon Derbyman is the editor. His policy is to work to short time-scales to ensure the news value of articles and thereby attract and hold a volatile readership. He is not keen on advertisement-linked features.
Gordon and Jill are of equal managerial status; both report to a managing director who oversees four other technical journals and whose policy is to give the editors full control over journal content.
Jill wants to persuade Gordon to run at least one major quarterly article to which additional advertising can be linked. She is now considering how best to obtain Gordon's agreement.

Dogwood Borough Council has decided to move all its currently scattered services to a new central office block. The director of administration, Ronald Morris, has the responsibility for planning this move and has the executive authority to decide the necessary allocation of office space.
He knows that whichever detailed office plan he prepares will be unpopular with one or other of the departments to be moved. They all value their current separate office identities. They are all determined to secure the most favoured office areas in the new block.
Having prepared what is, in his view, the most efficient office plan, Ronald has convened a meeting of the heads of the departments affected by the move. He has told them that the aim of the meeting is 'to attempt to reach a mutually acceptable allocation of office space in the new HQ' and is now planning his tactics for the meeting.

These two examples can now be examined against the four aspects of negotiating strength outlined above.

Decision-making power

In the first example, Jill (the manager wishing to achieve change) has no direct authority or decision-making power. Gordon, the editor, is able simply to reject her suggestion. In contrast, Ronald in the second example has the authority, if he wishes, to impose his office plan on the other departmental heads – though he has chosen to attempt a negotiated solution. In each case – if for opposite reasons – negotiation could have been a non-starter. To be successful in their negotiations, both parties need to recognise this possibility and plan accordingly.

In Jill's case, if she gives any impression that she is challenging or is resentful of Gordon's editorial authority, she will run the risk of his reverting to the role of autocratic editor and refusing to listen to her ideas. She must search for other forms of influence.

Ronald could have chosen not to negotiate. He is attempting this course, however, mainly because he would prefer to implement a plan that the departmental heads have accepted, rather than use his authority to override their probable objections. In handling the meeting he would be wise, though, not to appear to have surrendered this authority. He may need to remind the other managers that, if the going gets rough and they cannot agree, he will have no option but to impose his own plan. Part of his negotiating strategy, therefore, is to make positive use of his decision-making power, without necessarily having to exercise it directly.

In conventional collective bargaining, such as an annual pay negotiation, it is tacitly accepted that each party will suspend its powers of unilateral action while the negotiation proceeds. Yet both parties will be influenced by their separate assessments of their relative strengths. Similarly, when purchasing managers are negotiating prices with suppliers, both are influenced by their views on the extent to which the buyer might be able to obtain the goods from an alternative source. The buyer of a unique but essential product is in an exceedingly weak bargaining position – and will consequently wish, if at all possible, to conceal this dependency from the single supplier.

The power of influence

Negotiators are often influenced by other considerations than the pros and cons of the matter under discussion. It is under this heading that Jill, in particular, will need to plan her case. Can Gordon's likely opposition to her request be modified by other factors that he will perceive as offering benefits or carrying risks? This is where office politics sometimes intrude. If Jill thinks she is in better standing than Gordon with the managing director, she may be able to imply that rejection of her request might be viewed with disfavour. However, using actual or implied threats of this kind is a risky tactic which may generate resentment and obstruction. People respond more favourably to benefits than threats: as US sales trainers say, 'Sell it sunny side up'. So Jill's ploy is to remind Gordon that extra advertising pages will generate the revenue to provide for more editorial pages, to portray her quarterly advertisement-linked articles as an extra feature – not as an erosion of current editorial content, and to point out the interest to readers, not just to advertisers, of what she has in mind.

Ronald can afford to be much less concerned with his ability to influence. He can plan his negotiations against a background of ultimate authority and on the logic of his plans. He may, nevertheless, think about the advantage he may gain for the future by giving the departmental heads this opportunity to influence office plans. Among those affected is the director of finance. Ronald knows that this director is working on a new system for costing and allocating office overheads. This new system will affect Ronald's budget, and could be imposed by the finance director. Perhaps, thinks Ronald, by avoiding the imposition of the office plan he can put some credit 'in the bank' with the finance director, which may lead to a discussion of the new costing system rather than its imposition. More generally, he knows that all the managers will appreciate being given the opportunity of reaching a corporate agreement, and this will benefit the whole of his working relationship with them.

In managerial and trade union negotiations, their effect on long-term relationships is often an influential, if indirect factor. A purchasing manager may adopt an aggressive attitude in negotiating with a possible supplier, knowing that if the bargaining fails, the relationship ends. But two managers, or a manager and a shop steward, know that they have to maintain working contacts regardless of the outcome of any one negotiating episode. Consciously or unconsciously, they may moderate their bargaining positions to avoid damaging their long-term relationship. The introduction of internal trading has heightened the relevance of this factor and led, in some organisations, to the negotiating stance adopted by the in-house purchasers and providers, inflicting damage to working relationships. Operational departments that specify and 'buy' the services they need from support functions such as personnel or finance through the medium of service-level agreements have sometimes adopted a dictatorial approach, whereas the support units attempt to improve their internal trading results by exploiting loopholes in the specifications. The result is confrontational negotiation between purchaser and provider and a breakdown in the constructive, collaborative relationships that the organisation really needs. Failings of this kind may well result from inexperience in managing quasi-contractual working relationships, and the managers concerned would do well to study the type of relationship that many highly successful companies develop with their external suppliers and subcontractors. They encourage these sources to contribute their ideas about product or service improvements, and negotiations are concluded in a positive and constructive manner. The ongoing working relationship is seen as a form of partnership – not as a contest about which party can gain most advantage from the other.

The introduction of personal employment contracts can create tensions between managers and individual employees. When a manager meets an employee to negotiate the terms of a personal contract, both are aware that the tenor of the discussion – as well as its outcome – can affect their mutual attitudes. Some managers find it difficult to say no to an employee in these circumstances when, aside from the differing views about salary, the person is a well-liked and very co-operative member of staff. Will disagreement damage the longer-term relationship and the quality of day-to-day working contact? An alternative effect is for the employee to be reluctant to raise a matter of importance in case this causes the manager irritation. Both parties may consequently experience difficulty in handling the negotiating situation they find themselves in.

There is a legal presumption that the parties to a negotiation about a contract of employment have equal power and equal rights. Changes to an existing contract must be consensual, and either party is free to refuse to agree to the other's proposal. The risks of disagreement are also shared. The employer may lose the services of a valuable employee who resigns (or fails to join the company); the employee may risk losing a job if an untenable adversarial relationship develops. In real life, of course, matters are even more complicated. Both sides will want to establish or maintain a pleasant, informal working relationship. Factors that prevent agreement may derive not from their own decisions but from company policies or regulations. It is important for managers to have a clear idea of the objectives for the negotiation-type discussion and the outside limits of any concessions. They should also be prepared to explain, in impersonal, rational terms, *why* limits have to be drawn. 'I'm not prepared to pay you a salary of more than £20,000' sounds like a personal opinion, and may even be felt to imply some criticism. '£20,000 is as far as we can go within the company's salary structure' may still be a disappointing message, but it is less personal and cannot be construed as criticism.

In such situations, or when negotiating terms with outsourced staff such as freelances and self-employed project workers, it is helpful if managers work within a policy and stop to consider the likely effects on other staff of any agreements that they may reach. Company policies may be seen as restrictive by entrepreneurial managers, but those that permit reasonable freedom of action within broadly defined boundaries can also protect them from the adverse effects of what might otherwise be an array of inconsistent and incompatible individual arrangements. It may be possible, for example, to get a single freelance worker who is in a weak negotiating position to agree to a very low daily fee. But as soon as he or she discovers that others are paid more, resentment is likely to undermine the working relationship and erode commitment and quality.

The current trend towards substituting individual contracts for collective agreements allows for much greater recognition of the particular skills and performance of each employee. Yet in negotiating such contracts (or agreeing terms with outsourced staff), the wise manager always keeps in mind the value of achieving a pattern of pay and conditions across the whole workforce that can be explained and defended on rational grounds. The negotiations may be individual; the business objectives are corporate.

The strength of the case

None of these more general considerations of power and influence should divert the negotiators' attention from the efficacy of their specific arguments and objectives. There is certainly a risk that too great an emphasis on the 'political' dimension will result in a bad decision about the issue under negotiation.

Jill must clearly rely in the main on the strength of her proposals in sound business terms. This means that she must have all the evidence available to support her arguments – market trends, advertiser and reader responses, the practice of competitors, and cost and profit forecasts. The weaker the power position, the stronger the detailed case needs to be.

Ronald, too, should be able to show that he has recognised the departmental heads' needs and produced a solution that, although not satisfying all their separate objectives, produces a reasonable balance that makes overall sense. One of his reasons for deciding to negotiate rather than dictate is he has realised that almost every feature of his plan that will be objected to by one manager will be to another's advantage. His strategy, therefore, is not to set himself up against a united front of objectors, but to use their separate and differing views to counter each other's arguments. He is confident that by highlighting these differences, the logic of his own plan will emerge.

In internal trading, negotiations about the quality or cost of services should concentrate on the operational or business needs of the organisation – impersonal factors about which each party should have a common interest and be able to agree – rather than on considerations of winning or losing battles of power and influence. In negotiations about personal contracts, the manager should be able to explain his or her views as to what is acceptable by reference to the organisation's policies, standards, or core values, and not allow the discussion to become a personalised conflict of wills.

Determination

Negotiations are influenced by the determination or persistence of the parties. When trade unions present a claim consisting of several different items – say, for a pay increase, an extra day's leave, one hour off the working day, and a pension improvement – the experienced personnel professional will try to discover which of the items the union is most determined to achieve. It may be that one or other has been included as something of a makeweight, to be used more as a bargaining factor than as a real negotiating objective. Detecting the crunch issues helps to ensure that the negotiation makes progress, and that time and effort are not wasted treating more peripheral issues as though they are of critical importance. Similarly, the management may also need to let the union see that progress is more likely on some issues than others because of a determination to hold the line on one, or achieve a particular outcome on another.

Many managers have also experienced the effect of an individual employee's persistence in returning again and again with the same request – perhaps for a pay increase or for support in starting a course of professional study. On the first one or two occasions, and for sound reasons, the answer is (let us say) no. But after further repeated requests, the manager's resistance may be worn down and eventually the request is conceded, or some form of compromise is agreed. What can occur in such cases is that the manager's objective ceases to be the support of the right position from a policy viewpoint but becomes instead the simple avoidance of further personal hassle. This is, of course, a high-risk strategy for the employee, as it may be for anyone who decides to use persistence as a way of eroding initial resistance. The effect may be to generate resentment, a loss of patience, and a consequently unpleasant and negative outcome, so the strategy needs to be used with caution.

This is not to say that persistence has no place in negotiation. In intermanagerial situations, for example, it may well pay to draw back from what appears to be a fruitless attempt to achieve agreement before relationships become strained, and then return to the point with a more effective set of arguments. This is a point for Jill to keep in mind. If her first approach to Gordon runs into difficulties, she could close the discussion without making any concessions, but return to the issue a day or two later, having developed a perhaps more persuasive set of arguments. There is an important difference between determination and a stubborn refusal to compromise. Most negotiations involve some give and take on both sides. To persist in a refusal to alter one's opening position may achieve no more than a breakdown in negotiation. Lord Goodman, the internationally renowned lawyer, was once asked what he considered to be the single most important quality of the effective negotiator. He replied, 'The determination to achieve an agreement' – not, it will be noted, a determination never to compromise.

Key points

- Before embarking on negotiation there is a need to assess the parties' relative strengths.
- Strength is the power or influence that each can exercise over the final outcome.
- Power and influence may be indirect, affecting factors other than the immediate issues under negotiation.
- It may take four forms:
  - decision-making authority
  - the power of influence
  - the strength of the actual case
  - the determination or persistence of the negotiator.
- Influence may be negative – causing the other party damage – or positive – offering the other party benefit or advantage.
- The strength of the actual case can include its logical validity, its emotional appeal, and the degree of persistence and determination displayed in its pursuit.

———— 3 ————
Setting the Objectives

In planning a negotiation, an assessment of relative strength should be linked to the determination of objectives – the outcomes aimed for. To a large extent, the stronger one's position, the higher or more optimistic can be the objective. Commercial negotiators are often advised to define three possible settlement levels:

● the ideal, or best possible deal
● the expected settlement level
● the worst, though still just acceptable deal.

So a stationery supplier, negotiating next year's supply contract with a major customer, might set a figure of £150,000 as the ideal objective, £140,000 as a more realistic expected outcome, and £120,000 as the bottom line.

Meanwhile the buyer might be setting £100,000 as the ideal price, £115,000 as the expected outcome and £130,000 as the outside limit.

Assuming no other factors intrude, the logic of these figures is that the final settlement will fall between £120,000 and £130,000 – the overlap between the two parties' ranges of objectives.

This form of analysis provides a starting-point for considering objectives, but it is much too simplistic for many negotiations. In real life, things are rarely as clear cut, with factors other than price influencing the outcome, and with both parties aware of alternatives. An example illustrates this:

Sue Downs is the computer manager for a retail group. She is about to negotiate with Stockcom, a software company, for the supply of a computerised personnel records system. None of the packages on the market meets all her needs, but Stockcom has a package that, with some modifications, would be close to ideal. A technically similar package might be developed by another software house, but they have quoted nine months for design and delivery. Sue wants a system up and running well before then.

She has a budget of £35,000 to cover the purchase of the new system and initial staff training. If the cost is less, the saving can be carried over to next year for further computer enhancement. If the cost is higher, she will either have to make offsetting savings elsewhere in her department or seek top management approval to exceed her budget.

Price is not the only factor she has to take into account: delivery dates are important, and ideally she would like the system operational within two months – six months is her outside limit. She could compromise a little on technical specification if this eased any price or delivery problems. She has a choice, too, of negotiating for training to be done by Stockcom as part of a turnkey deal, or of handling training herself.

Two non-financial factors also affect her analysis of objectives. She has it in mind next year to make a case for upgrading her company's mainframe computer. If at all possible, therefore, she not only wants to avoid going to top management for a budget overspend this year but would also like to accumulate a budget surplus to help in arguing her case next year. Against this, the personnel and finance managers are pressing very hard to have a new records system installed as quickly as possible. They are already expressing criticism of the delay caused by her very thorough exploration of the software market.

Thus, in deciding the upper and lower limits for the outcome of her negotiation, Sue has to use her judgement – not just a statistical calculation – to balance a quite complex interaction between:

- price
- delivery
- specification – system features
  – training
- relationships – with top management
  – with colleagues.

She also has to consider the bargaining strength of the supplier and to set all this against an alternative of dropping Stockcom, changing the outside limit on delivery, and approaching the alternative supplier.

23

Deciding the top line

For the many negotiations in which more complex issues exist than the single factor of price it is more useful to identify a 'best achievable' top line than try to distinguish between an ideal and an expected outcome. This is the best outcome it is realistic to expect to achieve having taken all factors into account, including relative strength. It might well consist of a set of alternatives. In Sue's case, for example, there may be several permutations of price, delivery, and specification that would all be fully satisfactory. The most common failing in planning for negotiation is overoptimism about this achievable outcome. In negotiations with trade unions, for example, there is a tendency for managers to convince themselves that they have an irresistable case – based on business logic – for offering only a very modest pay rise; and that the unions will reluctantly accept this without resorting to any form of industrial action. A 'final offer' is eventually made, with managers confident of acceptance. Frustratingly, the unions then refuse to accept what managers felt was the overwhelming evidence to support the finality of the offer, and persist in pressing a higher claim – backed, perhaps, by strike action.

Similar overoptimism often infects other forms of negotiation. The personnel manager assumes that the office manager will agree to a new method of employee consultation because, from a personnel viewpoint, the new system is obviously better. A supplier assumes that the customer will not object too strongly to a price increase because the product has obviously been improved. A chief executive is convinced that the company need pay only a very modest sum in a negotiated settlement for an unfair dismissal, because to think otherwise would be admitting a greater degree of company blame than he or she is prepared to consider.

There is a common thread running through all these examples: a failure to consider the position from the other party's point of view. In pay negotiations, managers need to ask themselves how the union officials will justify a low pay settlement to their union members. The personnel manager needs to assess what the advantages of the new consultation system are from the production manager's viewpoint. The supplier should consider whether the product improvements are so relevant to the customer that they will overcome resistance to the price increase. The chief executive needs to look at the dismissal from the standpoint of the employee concerned.

The bottom line

Overoptimism about probable outcomes is often linked to a failure to give the bottom line adequate consideration – the worst outcome that would still just be acceptable. This failure carries two risks:

- An overrigid position will be taken by refusing to compromise or to consider alternative outcomes. A damaging breakdown in negotiations may then occur.
- Alternatively, once the ideal outcome has been shown to be unrealistic or unattainable, no prepared fall-back position has been identified, and an eventual agreement may be concluded that is worse than circumstances justify.

So identifying the bottom line may be more important than setting the original target. There may be a variety of possible satisfactory outcomes, so that flexibility in setting the best achievable target is essential. But there are usually some elements (costs, prices, standards) that must be set as outside, lower limits. In the software negotiations used as an earlier example, Sue might well decide that the total cost – whatever the precise package – must not exceed £28,000, and the outside limit for delivery is six months. Any package deal on which one or both of these limits is exceeded must be rejected.

Being clear about the bottom line is a necessary protection against being persuaded, in the heat of negotiations, to accept outcomes that inflict real damage, and that are worse in their effect than a possible breakdown in negotiations should the bottom line be held.

Credibility

It is obviously unwise to declare one's upper and lower limits when negotiations begin. The other party would then ignore the top line and concentrate on negotiating down to the bottom line as quickly as possible. In any event, some flexibility needs to be maintained, particularly during the joint exploration of possible outcomes. Unforeseen points or proposals may be raised that will require a quick reconsideration of one's limits. In Sue's case, for example, the supplier might offer a leasing deal instead of outright purchase, or might suggest staging payments over a three-year period. In both cases, a new bottom line would be worth consideration. This kind of variation to an original or expected position is often a feature of negotiations with an external supplier in an outsourcing situation.

There may come a point, however, when a decision and a statement should be made about this outside limit, such as, 'I cannot in any circumstances go beyond £28,000.' Or in a trade union negotiation, '6 per cent plus one day's extra leave has to be our final offer.' If credibility is to be sustained, 'final' must *mean* final. Companies have often undermined their own negotiating position by ill-prepared, overhasty or too frequent declarations that the bottom line has been reached, only to be forced by circumstances to waive this limit and agree to further concessions. Statements about limits' being reached, or about items' being non-negotiable, should be made with care and only in circumstances where the line can actually be held.

Winning and losing

It is common parlance to describe negotiations in terms of winning or losing. Popular media coverage often portrays the final outcome of an industrial dispute or a high-profile compensation case as being a victory for one side or the other, and rarely as a balanced compromise with benefits to both sides. Yet many writers and trainers urge negotiators to adopt a 'win/win' strategy. By this they mean attempting to reach agreements in which both parties feel they have achieved an advantageous outcome – as distinct from a 'win/lose' approach, in which each party sets out to defeat the other. In a win/win strategy, negotiation is seen as a collaborative rather than combative process.

This is a valuable attitude to adopt, particularly when negotiations are between people or institutions with a long-term working relationship – such as employer and trade union, or between managers in the same organisation. The damage to an important working contact that can be caused by one unpleasantly adversarial bout of win/lose negotiation can be considerable. It has to be recognised, however, that a genuine win/win strategy can be pursued only when both parties adopt this approach. Unfortunately for the theorists, some negotiators – particularly those who have not had the benefit of win/win training – see negotiation as a competitive, if not combative, process. An aggressive but adept negotiator will quickly take advantage of the good faith and helpfulness of an unwary or naïve win/win opponent.

There are also occasions when one party takes a wholly unacceptable position or presses a highly damaging claim, but circumstances prevent an outright rejection or a cessation of negotiation. In such cases there may be little alternative but to adopt a vigorous and assertive negotiating posture, and attempt to undermine the other side's position. This does not imply the adoption of an unpleasantly antagonistic personal manner: it does involve a determination not to be trampled on and not allow the other side, in effect, to win.

It is for these practical reasons that later chapters of this book include a few tactics, or responses, to aggressive negotiation that not all win/win theorists would be enthusiastic about.

Key points

- Negotiators need to identify a top line objective – the best achievable outcome – and a bottom line – the lowest, still acceptable outcome.
- Overoptimism about the probable outcome is often linked to a failure to consider the bottom line.
- Top and bottom lines may each consist of several alternative permutations of the issues under negotiation.
- Possible outcomes need to be considered from the other party's viewpoint as well as one's own.
- It is important to retain credibility by restricting statements about 'final offers' or sticking-points to *genuine* bottom lines.
- If possible, one objective should be to help the other party to feel satisfied with the outcome; but an aggressive or damaging claim has to be resisted with vigour.

Assessing the Other
Side's Case

Subjecting one's own case to critical scrutiny and deciding objectives and limits does not complete the preparation for a negotiating episode. It is also important to obtain as much information
as possible about the position to be taken by the other party. Three
main points are involved:

● what the other party is aiming for and their likely negotiating
  limits
● the facts and arguments they are likely to use to support their
  case
● whether there are any underlying and unstated issues or objectives, ie a hidden agenda.

An industrial relations example can be used to illustrate these
points:

> George Rogg, the personnel manager of an engineering company,
> received a letter from Harry Perkins, the TGWU district organis-
> er. The TGWU represented the company's maintenance workers,
> who included a small building section responsible for repairs to
> factory buildings. Harry's letter – which had been addressed to the
> chief executive, who passed it on – asked for an urgent meeting 'to
> resolve the unsatisfactory position arising from the use by the
> company of subcontractors to undertake repairs to the roof of
> Block A'. George knew that the maintenance shop steward was al-
> leging that the subcontractors were in breach of building safety
> regulations, and that there was bad feeling between the mainten-
> ance employees and the subcontractor's workforce. George
> thought the problem might also be that the subcontractor's em-
> ployees were not union members, though it was not clear from
> Harry's letter just what the TGWU would be seeking in any
> meeting.

George, therefore, replied to the TGWU letter, saying that the chief executive had a heavy diary and that it would help to speed the matter if Harry could provide a note of the particular issues he wished to discuss. This produced a phone call from Harry, from which it was evident that the complaint was that the maintenance section thought they could have done the roof repairs – probably on overtime – and objected to 'their work' being put out to contract. Overtime earnings loomed large in Harry's conversation.

Discovering the other party's aims

It is helpful in any type of negotiation, formal or informal, to know in advance what the other party wants to discuss and, in broad terms, what they are aiming for. In commercial negotiations this may generally be obvious – a meeting set up specifically, say, to negotiate an office rent review or to attempt to agree a price for some new equipment.

In many other negotiations, including informal intermanagerial episodes, the issue at stake may not become evident to the responding party until the discussion actually begins. This means that the party initiating the discussion has a marked advantage. He or she has been able to prepare a case: the other party has to respond without preparation. In the trade union example, George knows that Harry is an assertive and well-prepared negotiator. He does not want to be caught on the hop by being faced with an unexpected and perhaps well-documented claim – hence his follow-up suggestion to Harry before a meeting is fixed. This showed that earnings and job demarcation were the prime issues – not safety nor union membership – and George can now ensure that he is fully briefed on what will be the substance of any negotiations. He can make a reasonable assumption that the union's main aims will be protection of earnings and jobs.

The same principles can apply to a much more informal situation:

A typical managerial episode started with a line manager telephoning the purchasing manager and saying, 'May I come and see you about the policy on replacing office equipment?' Actually, the line manager had seen a new desk advertised and wanted to persuade the purchasing manager to buy one. Instead of just agreeing to the meeting, the purchasing manager asked, 'What particular aspect of the policy do you want to talk about? Is there anything specific you want to discuss?' It then became evident that the line manager's real aim was to have a new and better desk – regardless of any policy. This gave the purchasing manager the choice of preparing a response to the particular request if there was scope for discussion, or to save time by giving an immediate yes or no.

There is a tendency for managers with a very specific problem or request to wrap this up in a general enquiry about policy or procedure. Personnel managers, for example, are used to other managers' asking for a generalised interpretation of company policy on employee discipline, when what they really want to negotiate is legitimacy for a specific dismissal. A failure by the personnel manager to flush out the real case can lead to serious difficulties. A general interpretation is given to an apparently general enquiry; a dismissal occurs which is then the subject of a legal challenge; the line manager says that the action was taken on the personnel manager's advice; the personnel manager then realises that if the initial, general enquiry had been probed, a specific case would have been identified to which the generalised advice was not wholly appropriate. The better response to the first enquiry would have been 'It's difficult to give you a general answer that would fit all cases: what's your particular problem?'

The other side's facts and arguments

Checking what the issue is that the other party wants to pursue is only part of the preparation. It is even more helpful to know about the detailed facts and arguments they are likely to use, though this advantage is not necessarily one-way. In large, set-piece pay bargaining, it is not uncommon for the parties to exchange detailed written case statements setting out the statistical and other evidence on which their claims and positions are based. Each side takes the view that the other party can be influenced before the negotiations begin by seeing the strength of a well-researched and prepared case. Both parties want to avoid the confusion that can occur during negotiations if a mass of detailed statistics are introduced in a piecemeal way.

In less complex or more informal negotiations, this advance tabling of supporting data is very unusual. It is therefore helpful, having established what the issue is, to consider what facts and arguments the other party has, or is likely to advance, in support of their case. For George, in the trade union example, this means examining trends in the maintenance employees' overtime working and earnings, and any precedents that the union might quote about the allocation of repair work to subcontractors.

As with all preparatory assessments, it is important to look at the situation from the other party's viewpoint as well as from one's own. The question George should ask himself is, 'If I were Harry, what facts could I obtain to support my case, and how would I best use these in argument?' It is a common failing to think that one's own evidence is irrefutable and so to ignore or underestimate the conflicting data that the other party is bound to use.

A hidden agenda

Even after flushing out and assessing the specific issues to be dealt with, and the data that support the other party's case, there may still be in some circumstances an underlying issue that affects the quality and outcome of the negotiations. So, a standard question should be, 'Are there any other issues that explain or influence the way the other party develops their case?'

This was a factor in George's case. The first letter from the union was from Harry, the full-time district official, to the chief executive. This was unusual. Normally, Harry would be brought in only after the shop steward had exhausted discussions with George; normally, Harry's first contact would be with George – not with the chief executive. What lay behind Harry's departure from the normal procedure? It eventually transpired that the shop steward had reported to Harry that there had been a breakdown of mutual respect between George and the maintenance section. Harry's unorthodox letter to the chief executive was the opening shot in a fairly subtle union campaign to 'do something' about George.

Hidden agenda items also occur in commercial negotiations. A company negotiating an office cleaning contract with a local

31

authority may have its sights set on a later, larger street cleaning contract, and may, consequently, see the smaller contract almost as a loss leader. An office equipment supplier, negotiating for the sale of photocopiers, may be more interested in the longer run in obtaining a contract for the supply of stationery.

In managerial negotiations, other issues such as future relationships, later plans, personal prestige, and rivalry frequently lie just beneath the surface. Check-questions here, when approached by another manager with a proposal or request are, 'Why is this particular issue being raised at this time in this way?' Is the issue being raised to make a point about some other matter? What else might this manager be seeking than just the satisfactory resolution of the issue under direct discussion? These questions may seem to be negative and suspicious, but their intent is not to prevent a constructive resolution of the topics being debated. Rather, the aim is to ensure that the agreed solutions are not unwittingly biased by peripheral or unconnected factors.

Key points

- Establish what the other party's case is and what they are seeking to achieve.
- Probe whether specific problems or cases lie behind generalised questions or claims.
- Exchange factual data in advance of negotiations if this may helpfully influence the outcome or prevent delay and confusion during negotiation.
- Consider what facts and arguments the other party is likely to use in support of their case.
- Consider the possible existence of a hidden agenda – underlying issues that may influence the conduct and outcome of the negotiations.

5

Setting the Style and Scene

Having weighed up the bargaining position, set objectives, and assessed the nature of the other party's case, you can now turn your attention to the more detailed planning of the actual negotiation. An important issue is the general style or tone to be adopted: discursive or brisk, formal or informal, assertive or persuasive. The extent to which one party can set the style and the physical arrangements (room layout, seating plan, and the like) depends on which side is taking the initiative, and whether the other party is giving equal consideration to such planning. There has to be a good deal of flexibility in these preparations to cope with the possibility that the other party has planned a very different approach. However, many negotiators seem to pay relatively little attention to such factors, thus handling an advantage to the minority who do.

Six aspects generally need consideration, though some are of more relevance to formal negotiations between teams than to informal discussions between individual managers. These points are:

- the style or tone of the negotiations
- whom to involve – the composition of the negotiating teams
- the pace or timing of the negotiation
- the location – 'Their place or ours?'
- seating arrangements and the provision of refreshments
- how the negotiation is to be documented.

The style or tone

If both parties adopt the win/win approach discussed in the previous chapter, the style or tone of the negotiations will be firm but friendly, collaborative and constructive. Unless the other party is

33

known to adopt aggressive tactics, an emphasis on joint problem-solving rather than on winning debating points is by far the most effective. It would be very pleasant if it could be assumed that this style was universally adopted and, therefore, always appropriate. In reality, no such assumption can be made. There are circumstances in which other styles are needed. Consider this example:

Memorex is a computer bureau with a three-year contract to provide a staff wages and costing system for Doublegee – a glazing company. The contract has been running for 10 months. Doublegee recently wrote to Memorex terminating the contract forthwith on the grounds that the system was failing to perform to specification. Memorex challenged this: there had been a few minor problems but no serious breakdown. Memorex has heard on the industry grapevine that Doublegee has financial problems and is planning to cut its labour force and revert to a manual wages system. Memorex now submits a written claim for compensation for breach of contract. Doublegee counter-claim for alleged costs caused by system failures.

A meeting is arranged at Doublegee's offices to reach an agreed settlement. Given the tone of previous correspondence and telephone conversations, the Memorex team is not wholly surprised that the meeting starts with Doublegee's managing director launching an unpleasantly aggressive attack on Memorex's competence, tabling what he claims is chapter and verse for a string of system failures, and saying that unless Memorex drops its claim, he will pursue his counter-claim through the courts with technical evidence that will damage Memorex's professional reputation.

In planning for this negotiation, the Memorex team needs to prepare for just such an aggressive opening. They should avoid being provoked into an abusive rejoinder, but should establish very quickly that they have a strong case and are not going to be bounced into surrendering their claim. Their best response is probably to call Doublegee's bluff by saying that Doublegee's statement is an ultimatum, not a negotiable proposal, and that unless Doublegee is prepared to discuss the whole position constructively there is no point in proceeding with the meeting.

A more normal situation, particularly with discussions between managers and when negotiating with non-professionals such as shop stewards, is that the negotiation can go either way – constructive or combative – depending very much on the tone of the first few minutes. In these circumstances, the skilled negotiator always aims for a collaborative approach, and deliberately breaks the ice by a few minutes' friendly general small-talk before opening up the subject for discussion.

In considering negotiating style it is also important to take account of the experience and personality of the other party. For example, at some risk of generalisation it can be suggested that there are two broad types of trade union negotiator. There is an older group, almost all male, brought up in the hard school of assertive collective bargaining, often having begun their trade union activities as a shop steward and only later moving into full-time employment as a district or regional organiser. They are skilled in negotiating tactics, pragmatic rather than idealistic, drive hard bargains, but at the end of the day accept the inevitability of compromise. They are more concerned with practical outcomes than with underlying principles and are difficult to influence with theoretical arguments or intellectual analyses. They are used to, and may themselves adopt, an assertive bargaining style that includes a degree of personalised banter. Secondly there is a younger generation, often graduates, and with a growing proportion of women. They have a good understanding of business principles and management theory, and will use and respond to a well-constructed argument based on a rational analysis of relevant objective factors. Personalised banter – used traditionally to break the tension of a formal meeting – may be interpreted as frivolous, patronising, or discriminatory.

Managers who are inexperienced negotiators may also be influenced by stereotyped concepts of a hard-driven bargaining role. This can be seen in the way negotiations have been conducted in some organisations – particularly in the public sector – that have introduced internal 'trading' between operational and support functions. Operational managers with little or no commercial experience have now to negotiate service-level agreements with their financial, legal, and personnel departments for the supply of specialist support. They have an incentive to reduce their overheads by driving a hard bargain on support-service charges. At the same time, these support-service functions must now operate as 'business units', relying for their budgets on the volume of income they can generate from selling their services to operational departments. Managers in both roles may feel that the best way of protecting their financial interests is to adopt an uncompromising negotiating stance. The result can be a confrontational relationship between purchaser and provider that damages the corporate interests of the organisation as a whole. In reality, the most effective negotiating style in these circumstances is a collaborative one in which both parties accept the differences in each other's roles, recognise their shared interest in promoting their organisation's aims and values, and consequently build on common interests rather than emphasise differences.

It can also be helpful to attempt to identify the other person's style or preferred working methods in terms of Meredith Belbin's team typology,[1] which distinguishes between nine types or roles. The left-hand column gives the author's summary of Belbin's description of each type; the right-hand column sets out the author's interpretation of the implications for negotiators:

Role description	Negotiating implications
Plant: innovative, imaginative, unorthodox, clever, good at problem-solving, practical, impatient.	Does not take kindly to criticism, sees the big picture, may overlook incidental issues. Responds to bold new ideas. Can be combative but may well enjoy an intense, intellectually challenging argument.
Resource investigator: enthusiastic and extrovert, effective communicator, good natural and positive negotiator.	Potentially very receptive to constructive ideas. Good at developing other people's proposals. Responds to a collaborative negotiating style.
Co-ordinator: confident, mature, good at chairing meetings, clarifies complex situations, commands respect from colleagues.	Can be manipulative. Keeps track of multi-topic discussions and focuses on key issues. Can maintain emotional detachment. Responds to a calm, sensible, analytical approach.

36

Role description	Negotiating implications
Shaper: single-minded, argumentative, highly motivated, likes to win, assertive and impatient, with a strong drive to achieve positive results.	Likely to adopt a competitive approach. May be insensitive about the effect of his or her attitude on other people. May need to be challenged, but responds to firmly argued solutions (rather than analyses of difficulties).
Monitor-evaluator: serious, cautious, prudent, and shrewd, with a highly developed critical thinking ability.	Likely to need time to consider and accept new ideas. Will not be rushed. Responds to carefully constructed arguments that have a sound, logical basis.
Teamworker: perceptive and diplomatic, mild and supportive, a good listener but often indecisive, needing other people's support.	Uncomfortable in confrontational situations. Is very willing to consider ideas but may prevaricate about final agreement unless reassured that the outcome is satisfactory.
Implementer: practical, thorough and systematic, strong sense of loyalty to the organisation, good at turning ideas into practical action plans; not very creative.	Unlikely to offer spontaneous ideas. May display rigidity over a negotiating possibility unless convinced that it will serve the interests of the organisation. May be difficult to convince, but once committed to an agreement is very constructive about its implementation.
Completer-finisher: generally introverted, serious, intolerant of casual attitudes, great attention to detail, painstaking, concerned with following an idea through to practical implementation.	Wants to understand all the detail and practical implications of a proposal before agreeing. Likely to probe for errors, omissions, and difficulties. May react against any attempt at light-hearted easing of negotiating tension.

Role description	Negotiating implications
Specialist: single-minded interest in own area of expertise, self-motivated in relation to own specialism; a useful source of specific knowledge but not an all-rounder.	Interprets everything from own specialist viewpoint. Does not respond to arguments based on a broad picture. Needs to have technicalities explained, and arguments should be slanted to focus on implications for the specific area of expertise.

Tailoring the style and emphasis of negotiation to the experience and personality of the other party can have a very significant effect on the eventual outcome. It is, of course, easier to do this when negotiating with colleagues whose personal characteristics are known than it is when meeting other people for the first time across the negotiating table. In that case, however, it pays to be very aware of the personality factor and to be ready to change one's approach if the other party is unresponsive to the initial style.

Whom to involve

Informal managerial negotiations are normally between individuals, not teams. Yet one-to-one bargaining has its drawbacks, particularly if one manager is a markedly more dominant personality than the other, or has significantly more negotiating experience. In such cases, the less confident manager should think of involving an additional person.

> Leo Scott, a young and recently appointed personnel manager, wanted to talk to May Biron – a cynical, 55-year-old divisional head – to persuade her to use psychometric tests in the selection of graduate trainees. Leo had already had one very unsatisfactory talk with May on another topic, in which his ideas had been swept aside with little discussion. This time, when ringing May to make a date for their discussion about tests, he added: 'I'll bring Bert Robinson with me – he can help us with the information about

costs.' Bert was one of Leo's section heads; the real and effective reason for this involvement was to reduce the dominance that May could achieve in a one-to-one discussion.

In industrial relations, it is not uncommon for the trade union side to field a sizeable team – a union official, perhaps, supported by a stop stewards' committee. It is unwise for a single manager to attempt to negotiate alone with such a team. Negotiation demands a high level of concentration and quick thinking and it is difficult for one person to maintain full attention to everything that is said, and to detect every nuance in the discussion. This does not mean that the management team must equal the trade union in size. Indeed, to go beyond a fairly small number runs the risk of poor co-ordination between team members and the possibility that differing views might emerge within the team as negotiations proceed. Many experienced negotiators express a preference for three members in a team, and certainly no more than five.

The composition of a team is also important. If difficulties are expected, it may be advisable to be ready to handle the negotiation on a staged basis. In wage bargaining, for example, the management team might consist, in the first instance, of the personnel manager supported by two of his or her staff. If an impasse is reached, a second, higher-level team may then be used, consisting perhaps of the managing director, the finance director, and the personnel manager. At least one person should be involved in both stages to ensure continuity and to prevent the other side's misquoting things said at the first stage.

Within the team, thought needs to be given to each person's role. In a team of three, for example:

- one will act as leader and take a constructive, problem-solving stance
- another will take a harder line, challenging the other party's assertions and generally pointing out the difficulties caused by their claims
- the third member can act as 'sweeper', observing the reactions of the other team, checking progress, and bringing in any points missed by the other two members.

39

Pace and timing

The timing and pace of negotiation can have a major influence on the outcome. If a dispute has blown up very quickly about an issue on which emotions run high – such as a fatal accident at work – it may be as well to slow the pace of discussions to allow time for a highly-charged atmosphere to grow calmer. Achieving some delay in such circumstances requires very delicate handling. It is all too easy for a dispute on one issue (such as safety regulations) to be converted into a second dispute about the management's alleged time-wasting or reluctance to talk. One way of proceeding is to suggest to the other party that a fact-finding exercise would be of use to both sides before formal negotiations begin.

It has become a well-established ploy in civil actions for compensation or damages for the lawyers to enter into protracted correspondence before any effective bargaining occurs about out-of-court settlements. The theory is that the claimants will become so frustrated by lengthy delays that they will eventually agree to a much more modest settlement – simply to bring the matter to a conclusion – than they initially thought acceptable. The morality of such a tactic is obviously questionable. It may be, too, that far from weakening the resolve of claimants, blatant time-wasting may strengthen their determination to succeed.

Although deciding on a slow or fast pace is a matter for judgement in each case, one general guideline can be suggested: to move quickly rather than slowly when the other party's position is a strong one. Indeed, at the extreme, there may be a case for conceding a claim or request without negotiation if the other party's argument cannot sensibly be challenged. Some managers resist any claim by a trade union as a matter of reactive routine. They would gain more respect if, on occasions when the union's proposal was clearly well-founded, they said yes quickly and cheerfully – rather than being dragged to an eventual reluctant acceptance after time-consuming negotiation.

Location

There is often a choice of location for a negotiating meeting. For example, in the case of negotiations between managers or companies, in whose office should the meeting be held? Should a negotiating session with trade unions be held in the management offices or on neutral ground such as a hotel conference suite? With experienced negotiators, location should make no difference, but many people find that the negotiating environment can influence their confidence and attitudes. This does not imply that, given a choice, it is always best to select home territory.

A very experienced personnel manager in a large company was renowned for his persuasive ability in meetings with his managerial colleagues. Explaining his working methods to a new secretary, he said: 'Whenever I have meetings with other managers, however junior, I always try to hold them in their offices, not mine. It makes them feel I have put myself out a bit, and shown more of an interest in them. So I start one-up!'

When the negotiations involve complex issues, it may be helpful to hold them on home ground so as to have ready access to supporting documents, and possibly to call in additional team members as the discussions progress. Certainly, when such negotiations are located away from base, very careful thought needs to be given to the composition of the team and what files should be taken.

Large-scale, set-piece pay bargaining is sometimes conducted on neutral ground to avoid any implicit advantage for the side 'owning' the location. Even at a less formal level, it may be a good move to ask the union side if they would like the meeting held somewhere other than on the company's premises. It demonstrates an open, even-handed approach – and the outcome is quite likely to be a union suggestion to use the company's conference room.

Seating and refreshments

The seating plan for a negotiation can influence or reflect the participants' attitudes quite markedly. At its simplest, discussions between people sitting opposite one another at a very wide table tend to be more confrontational than if they are sitting next to one another in an informal group.

41

The conventional layout for a formal bargaining session is the 'across-the-table' format. Each team takes one side, with the two parties' leaders sitting directly opposite one another in the centre of the two long sides of the table. It is a format that many people feel comfortable with, because it emphasises the separate identity of each side, and each has its own territory. On the other hand, it encourages a competitive us-and-them style, and is consequently not the best format for a negotiation in which one objective is to break down unnecessary attitudinal barriers between those involved.

For the more informal, collaborative approach, a round table is far better – or even a grouping of comfortable armchairs around a low table.

Ed Reeve, the personnel manager referred to in the last example, also explained to his new secretary how he liked to arrange the few meetings he held in his own office. 'If I'm telling someone rather than asking,' he said, 'I stay behind my desk. Otherwise I always take them over to the coffee table, and put them in the deepest, softest armchair. It's very difficult to be belligerent when you are sunk into the upholstery, holding a cup of coffee.'

Occasionally, even in formal meetings, an unconventional seating plan may be contrived.

In one union negotiation, the management knew that the union official would take an aggressive line, whereas the senior shop steward was known to be much more conciliatory. Letting the union team sit down first, the management leader then chose a chair at the table immediately opposite the senior steward, instead of in the centre facing the union official. In the ensuing negotiation, the union official frequently had difficulty in catching the management leader's eye, whereas the management leader was able to bring the senior steward into the discussion far more easily than if a conventional seating plan had been adopted.

The party hosting the negotiations (or taking the lead in organising them if they are held on neutral territory) is expected to make some arrangements for refreshments. Providing light refreshments is an integral part of the formal negotiating ritual. Even when two managers are meeting informally, the 'host' omitting to offer a cup of something mid-morning or afternoon may well be taken as a significantly unfriendly sign: 'He was too mean even to offer a coffee!'

But a refreshment break can be used for more purposes than mere compliance with normal office courtesies. A pause for a cup of tea can be very helpful in lowering the emotional temperature if tempers have begun to rise. It can provide an opportunity for a quiet conversation between the two team leaders, or between the individual 'fixers' on each side. More deviously, the arrival of refreshments may – if the timing can be arranged unobtrusively – just happen to coincide with the other side's leader's launching into a powerful peroration. There is nothing more deflating than the sudden rattle of cups as the door opens for the tea trolley. Delaying refreshments may also be an effective way of encouraging more rapid progress.

A negotiation between two company teams about a supply contract was getting badly bogged down in conflicting detail. One o'clock arrived with no conclusion having been reached on even the preliminary point of quantity discounts. The purchasing company's team leader then said: 'We've laid on a buffet lunch for 1.15 in the next room, but I think we ought to reach a decision on discounts before we break, otherwise we shall all lose the thread of our arguments.' This ploy had been agreed within the company's team before the meeting started, so they were quite relaxed about the delay, but by 2.15 the other firm's team were getting extremely restless and very eager to settle.

Documentation

Are minutes or other records of the meeting to be kept? If so, by whom and in what form? The point is an important one, because it is not unknown for an oral agreement to be reached within a negotiating meeting only for the settlement to fall apart later when the two parties have a different understanding or recollection of what was said and of the details of the agreement.

The extreme in minute-keeping is the verbatim record, in which everything said in the negotiations is either tape-recorded or taken down by shorthand writers. It is a practice sometimes used in national collective bargaining. It seems to have been introduced when neither party would accept the other's summary of what had been said, and because of disputes as to who had said what during very protracted negotiations. Apart from the cost and voluminous paperwork this method involves, it can also back-fire on some of the participants when their casual comments are later put into cold print and circulated widely among union members. One leading employer, for example, made an off-the-cuff comment (intended humorously) at a meeting of the now defunct Burnham Committee for teachers' pay that the annual conference of the National Union of Teachers reminded him of a chimpanzees' tea party. Set out in the formal minutes, this led to accusations by teachers that he thought they were no better than monkeys – not a helpful step in securing agreement on a very modest pay offer.

Normally, then, verbatim records cannot be recommended. The important thing about any effective negotiation is its outcome – the agreement – and not the to and fro of argument that has led to this conclusion. There is, consequently, a good deal to be said for a written record that says little more than who was present, a brief summary of the opening positions of each side, and a full description of what was eventually agreed. This type of record does not require a formal minute-taker. One of the team can be deputed to keep a note of the meeting and, if necessary, clear this in draft with an opposite number in the other team before it becomes the formal record.

A fuller private record may be helpful, recording in complex negotiations the possibly different views or emphases of members of the other side, plus a note of points that emerged in discussion but did not figure in the final agreement. But a private record of this kind should be kept as a background aid, and not be sprung on the other party as a secret weapon.

A good method of recording the outcome of informal, managerial negotiations is for the manager taking the initiative in the discussion to confirm the outcome in a memo: 'Just a short note to confirm that we agreed yesterday to . . .'

Key points

- Negotiations are influenced by their style and pace, by the composition of the negotiating team, and by the arrangements for seating, refreshments, and documentation.
- Effective negotiators aim for a collaborative style but are prepared for confrontation.
- The style of negotiation also needs to take account of the background and personality characteristics of the other party.
- Other than in very formal negotiations, a team of three to five is advisable.
- Negotiations should be avoided while emotions are running high; but delay for its own sake is normally counterproductive.
- Inexperienced negotiators feel more confident on home ground, but for major, formal negotiations, the use of a neutral location may be desirable.
- Seating plans can be used to reinforce either a confrontational or a collaborative mode.
- Providing refreshments is not just a matter of common courtesy: refreshment breaks can be used to make progress in negotiations.
- Some record of the outcome of negotiations, however informal, is desirable in order to ensure a common understanding of what has been agreed.

Reference

[1] BELBIN, R. MEREDITH. *Management Teams.* London, Butterworth-Heinemann, 1981.

6

Setting the Agenda

No negotiation can be effective unless the two parties have a common understanding of what it is they are discussing, why it is being discussed, and what each is seeking to achieve. This may seem obvious, yet misunderstandings about the content or purpose of negotiations are common causes of difficulty.

The personnel manager of an insurance company received a request from the local trade union branch for a meeting 'to discuss the unsatisfactory situation in the computer room'. Because of previous complaints about ventilation, he assumed that this request also referred to environmental problems, and in preparation for the meeting he arranged for the building services engineer to carry out a series of checks on temperature and humidity. He then started the meeting by saying that he realised there had been problems in the past, but that recent checks had shown that a stable environment had now been achieved. It then transpired that the trade union wanted to talk about the layout of desks and VDUs, and their fears about a possible reorganisation had been exacerbated by seeing the engineer in the room. The subsequent discussion was then adversely affected by the personnel manager's having failed to prepare for the real issue, and by the trade union side's being suspicious of the management's intentions.

It would clearly have been wise for the personnel manager to have clarified the subject matter of the meeting beforehand. It would also have been better for him to have invited the trade union to speak first when the meeting began.

There are two aspects to agenda-setting:

- formally defining and agreeing with the other party what the discussion is about
- informally influencing the substance and character of the discussion.

The formal agenda

Even when negotiation is at its most informal – for example, two managers meeting to consider a matter of mutual interest – the effective manager establishes, in advance where possible, what the subject matter is.

Ed Reeve, the personnel manager referred to in the previous chapter, was well aware of this and would often try to obtain an advantage by initiating a meeting without explaining the real reason. For example, when he wanted to obtain the finance director's agreement to a budgetary change, he would ring the director and ask 'May I drop in on you this afternoon? I want your advice on a small point.'

Until he spotted the ploy, the finance director used to agree, only to be confronted with an extremely well-prepared and skilfully presented case for something rather more than a minor concession.

In response to such a request for a meeting, the director would now say: 'What's it about? I'm a bit pushed for time this afternoon so if you spend a couple of minutes on the phone now to fill me in, we can probably clear it more quickly when we meet.'

At the formal level, defining the subject matter of negotiations is often so important that it may itself be the subject of negotiation. The media sometimes make caustic comments about the time taken in national trade union disputes, or in international diplomacy, in 'talks about talks'. Although this may seem a time-wasting activity, it may be crucial for the success of the final negotiation. In an industrial relations pay dispute, for example, a subsidiary issue may arise about the dismissal of unofficial strikers. Both sides may want to make progress on the pay talks, but the trade union sees reinstatement of the dismissed employees as a pre-condition, whereas the employers are adamant that these dismissals are irreversible. The only way of breaking the deadlock is to have discussions about what is to be discussed – and, perhaps, how these discussions might be aided by the involvement of a third party such as the Advisory, Conciliation and Arbitration Service (ACAS).

In commercial negotiations, and in collective bargaining at company level, a simple exchange of correspondence is all that is needed. A meeting will be arranged, and the party initiating it will

47

write to the other saying: 'This letter confirms the arrangement for us to meet (date, time, place) to discuss (subject) with a view to reaching agreement about (objective).' Any potential misunderstanding about the nature of the meeting can then be cleared up by telephone or further correspondence – the aim in all cases being to start the negotiations with a shared view of their purpose.

Influencing the agenda

The first main speaker in a negotiating session has some advantage in being able immediately to influence the tone of the meeting and the sequence or emphasis given to the various aspects of the subject under discussion. The party initiating the claim or request usually takes this advantage, because it is logical for them to open the proceedings by stating their case. This does not mean that they should be allowed to introduce issues outside the already agreed agenda, but it does give them a scene-setting capability to influence the way the discussion will develop – the informal agenda.

It is, therefore, advantageous to claim this opening role if one wants to set the scene, rather than just respond. There is also a way of avoiding the simply reactive role, even when the other party must obviously be given the right of opening the formal negotiations. Ed Reeve's normal way of starting a negotiating session with his trade union officials illustrates this:

> The union had submitted a claim for an increase in the overtime premium, and Ed had set up a meeting with them to discuss this. Conventionally, management would open such a meeting by turning to the trade union leader and saying: 'We are meeting to consider your claim for higher overtime payments, so perhaps you could begin by explaining your claim.'
>
> This was not Ed Reeve's way. He liked to get in first. So his opening remark was: 'We are meeting to consider your overtime claim so we'll ask you to bat first. But before we start, it might be helpful if I just sketch in the background so that we are all in the same picture.' He then went on briefly to remind the union of the history of the current overtime arrangements and current overtime costs. dropping a hint that a joint study of unit costs might be a useful precursor to any change, and gently undermining the case he expected the union to have prepared. The phrase 'before we start' prevented an immediate union objection to management speaking first.

48

In managerial discussions, a similar technique can be used. The finance director faced with the equivalent of a well-prepared Ed Reeve making a bid for an improved budget could prevent Ed from dictating the course of the meeting by making an early interruption: 'Before we go any further, I would find it helpful to remind ourselves of last year's discussions . . .'

Despite initial efforts to define or influence the agenda, negotiations sometimes become bogged down in a confused discussion in which arguments become repetitive or lose sight of what each party is striving to achieve. This is particularly liable to occur when one party has a strong sense of grievance about the topic under discussion, and becomes more concerned with expressing these feelings than with working towards a solution; nor is it uncommon when dealing with inexperienced negotiators who have not fully prepared their case.

Three questions are useful in these circumstances to bring the negotiations into focus:

- 'We fully understand your views on this issue, but what are you actually asking us to do?'
- 'Are we right to think that the main point you want us to consider is x?'
- 'Is it clear that the main point we are making is y?'

Key points

- To be effective, the parties to negotiation need a common understanding of what is to be discussed and why.
- The subject, scope, and purpose need therefore to be agreed before negotiations commence.
- For formal negotiations, this definition of the agenda should be in writing.
- The progress of a negotiation is influenced significantly by the first speaker.
- One way of securing this opening position is to volunteer a brief rehearsal of the background before full negotiations begin.
- Confused negotiations need re-focusing by a restatement of each party's key points.

7

Probing the Other Side's Case

Once negotiations are under way, three things need to be kept continually in mind:

- that the ultimate objective is to achieve an agreed outcome or solution, but that . . .
- . . . before making concessions, the other party's case should be rigorously probed or tested (and possibly weakened) and . . .
- . . . every reasonable opportunity should be taken to strengthen one's own position.

The first point lies behind every chapter of this book. This chapter looks at the second of these points – the need to test the validity of the other side's position. The next chapter deals with strengthening one's own case.

Exposing flaws

It is rare for one party to a negotiation to have a totally unanswerable case – though it is much less rare for a negotiator to *think* that this is so, and common for arguments to be presented as worthy of immediate acceptance. Flaws in a case may be intentional distortions, or may result from inadequate preparation or an unconscious assumption of being in the right. Negotiators are too often convinced by the force of their own arguments and consequently it is essential for the other party that these arguments are rigorously probed. Particular points to look for are as follows.

Errors of fact

No statement such as '10 per cent of deliveries have been two days late' or 'increases in clerical staff earnings have fallen behind the rise in the RPI (retail price index)', should be allowed to pass unchallenged. If these points are important to the negotiation, the party making such statements should be asked to produce the hard evidence to substantiate them.

Omissions of fact

It is normal for a negotiator to build a case on correct, but only partial, data. So, 10 per cent of deliveries may well have been late, but the period under analysis included an unmentioned rail strike which distorted the statistics. Negotiators need to ask themselves – and if necessary the other party – 'Is that the whole story? What other facts may be relevant?'

In a national negotiation about fire-service pay, figures were given of the numbers of long-service firefighters who had resigned during the previous six months. This was quoted as evidence that men were leaving the service because of low pay. What was omitted were figures for the equivalent resignation rates over the previous five years. When these were produced it was evident that there had been no significant recent change in the resignation rate.

Misuse of statistics

Perhaps the most common misuse of statistics is to quote averages or percentages for a very small number of cases, or to use averages to conceal a very wide range of actual data. Averages (or the arithmetical mean) should often be challenged by calling for details of the number of cases, the range of data, and the median and mode positions.

Three examples illustrate how cases can be distorted unless the full facts are produced:

> The manager of a local authority housing department was seeking a reduction in the internal charges for personnel services from the

in-house payroll unit. Her case was that the standard in the service-level agreement for the time to process changes in individual pay rates was not being met. 'The standard is three working days,' she said, 'but the average has been 5.1.' The payroll manager was able to produce data to show that the average had been completely distorted during the past month by a major change in the bonus formula which had not been provided for when the original service specification had been agreed. If this exceptional event was set aside, the three-day average had been met in all other cases. The figures were: 140 normal cases @ three days; 100 exceptional cases @ eight days – giving an arithmetical average of 5.1 days.

An employee who was seeking a pay rise used, as one argument, a claim that the section he headed had achieved a 25 per cent reduction in customer complaints during the previous 12 months. The manager checked the actual figures and had to point out that, whereas any such trend was to be applauded, a reduction in the number of complaints from eight to six was not so remarkable as to justify an increase in salary.

A trade union officer, making a case that one group of technicians was worse paid in terms of gross earnings than a comparator group in another department, quoted the average earnings in the two groups as £310 and £325 respectively. An analysis of the payroll showed these figures for the arithmetical mean to be accurate. But the same analysis also showed that the *median* earnings for the groups were, at £320, identical. The figures were:

Group 1:		Group 2:	
2 × £250		6 × £300	
8 × £305		10 × £320	
5 × £320		1 × £400	
10 × £322		1 × £450	
Mean:	£310.40	Mean:	£325
Median:	£320	Median:	£320

In addition to quoting this median, the company manager also argued that the first group was better paid, because 92 per cent received more than £300 compared with only 66.6 per cent in the second group.

Faulty logic

Firm conclusions are often drawn from weak bases. 'Salaries are too low because staff are leaving for higher-paid jobs elsewhere'

– but that is normal: why should anyone leave for a lower salary? And unless one's own organisation is the highest-paying in the industry, there will always be some firms paying more. Any key conclusion drawn by the other party should be examined closely against the basis on which it has been drawn.

Appeals to emotion

With a weak case (in terms of fact or logic) it is normal for negotiators to fall back on emotional appeals. 'OK, so the company is short of cash and subject to fierce overseas competition – but it is still unfair that our members should be paid below the industrial average'; or 'Wouldn't your company's reputation benefit from being seen to be generous, even though our client has no legal rights?' Concepts of fairness and reputation can be very powerful influences, and may well justify a case that is otherwise weak. It is not a matter of rejecting all such appeals. It is important, though, to recognise the basis of such arguments and consider them carefully and rationally before making concessions.

Testing the other side's case for flaws is best done by asking questions rather than by making counter-statements. Questions are less threatening but more revealing. It is much more effective, for example, even if the answer is known, to ask: 'On how many cases is your average figure based?' than to state: 'Your average figure is meaningless.' Apart from the direct questioning of facts (How many? How much? When?), more general, but useful, probing questions, are:

- Could you explain your thinking about that more fully?
- We don't follow the logic of your argument: could you put it a different way?
- Isn't what you are really saying x? If so, how do you justify it?
- Could you explain the connection between x and y?

Testing credibility

It would be wrong to suggest that attempts should be made in *all* negotiations to undermine the credibility of the other side's leader. His or her standing with the team's members may justifiably be very high and, in that case, any attempt at belittlement would be counter-productive. The team will rally to their leader's support.

There are occasions, however, when it may be judged that a vociferous and aggressive teamleader does not have the unquestioned support of his or her team. In such cases, it is worthwhile trying to pin any flaws in the other party's case personally on the leader. If the team's confidence in their leader's credibility can be sapped, their ability to secure their original negotiating objectives will be markedly weakened. An industrial relations example illustrates this:

> A trade union team was meeting with management to pursue a claim that an employee dismissed for a disciplinary offence should be re-instated. The trade union team consisted of a very aggressive and self-opinionated district official and five much less assertive shop stewards. All the talking was done by the district official, who adopted an uncompromising stance backed, as he claimed, by case-law arising from a recent decision of the Employment Appeals Tribunal. His team was obviously impressed by his apparent knowledge of the law, and the management allowed the argument in favour of re-instatement to be built very firmly on the legal position, although in reality the issue was influenced almost entirely by local considerations.
>
> The personnel manager then chose the moment to say: 'You would be right in your argument, George, except that you are out of date on your case-law. Didn't you know that the House of Lords overturned the EAT decision last week? I've got *The Times* law report here, if your team would like to see it.' The effect was of course seriously to undermine the shop stewards' confidence in their district official's competence.

The innocent little question 'Are you sure about that?' is a very powerful way of raising doubts about an opposing negotiator's credibility. It does no damage if they can substantiate what they have been saying, but saps both their own confidence and their standing in the eyes of their team if their argument is flawed.

Key points

- The other side's case should be tested for:
  - errors or omissions of fact
  - misuse of statistics
  - faulty logic
  - emotional appeal.
- The credibility of the other side's leader may need to be undermined, provided that this does not result in a defensive reaction.

8
Strengthening One's Own Case

The strength of one's own negotiating position depends partly on the power to make unilateral decisions (a point discussed in Chapters 1 and 2), partly on the validity of the arguments one uses, and partly on the way these arguments are developed. This chapter is concerned with taking or making opportunities to strengthen one's position in the course of negotiating. There are two main aspects: identifying, and reminding the other party of, possible sanctions; and improving the impact of one's arguments and proposals through a variety of negotiating tactics.

Sanctions

Sanctions are concerned with power. They are the influences external to the details of the topic under discussion that may assist one party or the other to get its way. In the extreme, they are the means used to force a conclusion if negotiations fail.

For instance, a commercial negotiation to settle a claim for the increased costs of a building contract, caused allegedly by the client's failure to provide an adequate specification, may be settled by an arbitrator or the courts if the two parties fail to agree between themselves. The party which thinks it has the best case may well use the threat of arbitration or court action as a negotiating sanction. Its negotiating tactics will include reminding the other party from time to time of the delays and costs involved if the claim is pursued through the courts, and that the probable outcome will favour the claimants.

In industrial relations, trade unions sometimes use the threat of strike action as a sanction. 'Negotiate reasonably,' is the message, 'or we'll walk out.' The employers' counter may be another form of sanction – the threat of a factory closure or job losses. In internal trading systems, many service-level agreements include a clause stating that in the event of a failure to agree between the provider and purchaser, the matter will be referred to the chief executive. Whichever party considers its case to be the stronger may use this threat of a reference to top management as a potential sanction, judging that the other party will not want to risk being found unreasonable by the chief executive. Constructive negotiation is not conducted best as an exchange of threats. People react against duress. But what *is* sometimes needed is the occasional reminder that there are certain realities about the situation and that, if all else fails, the use of a sanction will be inevitable.

So the negotiator's approach in a building contract case was: 'We would much prefer to reach an agreed conclusion but, if you persist in the line you are currently taking, we would have to think seriously about referring your claim to arbitration. Our legal advice is that while we would be ready to make some modest concessions – which we are still prepared to discuss – it is highly improbable that an arbitrator would give full support to your claim. Do you really want to have the delay and cost of an arbitration reference? Wouldn't it be better to try to make progress on an agreed basis?'

Chapters 13, 14, 15, and 19 take a more detailed look at the particular sanctions available in managerial, commercial, and industrial relations negotiations. For now, the following check-list sets out the principal types of sanction that a negotiator can consider:

- *financial sanctions:* increased costs resulting from stoppages or delays, changes to specifications, loss of business
- *legal sanctions:* the delays of the legal process; arbitration or compensation awards; injunctions to prevent action occurring; declarations of rights
- *personal or organisational reputation:* damage to the individual or company image caused by apparent intransigence, insensitivity, disregard of customer relations, or incompetence
- *self-regard:* 'loss of face' resulting from failure to conclude a satisfactory agreement (no real damage to the organisation's or individual's formal or business interests may be involved, but the person's self-confidence and pride are hurt)

● *emotional sanctions:* appeals to a negotiator's sense of fairness or sympathy, regardless of the strict merits of a case.

Tactics

Three tactics may be used to strengthen a negotiator's position during the bargaining process:

● the introduction or exclusion of new issues
● attaching conditions to concessions
● the use (and misuse) of emotion.

The introduction of new issues

In the discussion of agenda-setting in Chapter 6, the general principle was made that the subject and scope of a negotiation should be defined in advance. There are occasions, however, when the introduction of new issues may be advantageous. This is probably easier to achieve in an industrial relations context or between managers – situations in which both parties have an ongoing involvement in many matters other than the immediate point under discussion – than in a commercial setting. For example:

A local authority personnel manager was meeting with the trade union UNISON to consider the union's claim for a higher level of car allowances. She had agreed this as the subject for the negotiations, and the claim was a simple one – that those staff who used their own cars at work, and whose cars were over 1½ litres in engine size, should be paid at a higher rate than the existing allowance.

By agreeing to discuss the matter, the personnel manager had given an indication of some willingness to make a change – otherwise she would just have said that the authority was not willing to make any alteration to the current allowance. She decided to use the claim, however, to widen the discussion to include two new issues that the management wished to pursue. One was the use of leased cars for high business-mileage users (with a charge for private usage) as an alternative to car allowances. The other was the introduction of a more rigorous system of vetting expense claims.

By widening the scope of the negotiations, she was able to offset the costs of a small concession on car allowances by the agreed introduction of cost-saving measures on high mileage users and general expense payments.

This type of 'packaging' of issues – which may be possible to achieve only by introducing new elements once the negotiations are under way – offers more scope for compromise and trade-offs than the more intense bargaining involved in keeping strictly to single issues.

Another use of new issues is to provide a diversion or breathing-space if things are going badly. Another industrial relations case illustrates this:

The managing director (MD) of a publishing company was meeting the NUJ chapel (the journalists' union branch) to consider a claim for increased annual leave. The union had prepared a much better case than the MD expected, and produced a great deal of evidence about other firms that showed how far theirs had fallen behind the rest of the industry.

Realising that there could be no real argument about these comparisons, the MD stopped the discussion in its tracks by saying: 'Before we go any further, I have to say that this opens up the whole question of productivity. We really can't go on talking about more leisure time when what this company dearly needs is much more commitment to output while we are at work!'

This did not cause the union to withdraw their claim, but it prevented the MD's being driven into a bargaining corner and gained him time to consider his position.

Of course, the other side may also use this tactic, and it is then a matter of judgement as to whether to accept the new point or firmly to reject it on the grounds that 'That isn't what we agreed this meeting would be about.' A related tactic that cannot be recommended, but which may be tried by a confrontational negotiator, is to use a personal attack as a diversion. The object is to throw the other party off balance – possibly by making them lose their temper – and so lose the thread of what was probably a strong argument.

In one intermanagerial discussion, John Gordon, a sales manager, was trying to persuade Stan Hollett, the production manager, to change the production schedule. Stan was patiently resisting John's pressure, and embarked on an explanation of the whole production-planning process and the high costs of an unplanned scheduling change. John went on the attack. 'That's your trouble, Stan, you're just a narrow-minded mechanic,' he said fiercely. 'All you ever do is to defend the perfection of your damned computerised programme. When are you going to learn that there are real, live customers out there!'

If Stan was inexperienced, he might well have lost the thread of his argument at this by rising to the bait and defending his personal reputation. Instead, he used the effective negotiator's ploy of refusing to allow himself to be provoked, and deflected the attack with a good-humoured grin and a light-hearted comment about the honourable trade of the mechanic.

It may take much self-control not to react to a personal attack, but if one's negotiating strength is not to be weakened such attacks need to be recognised for what they are: a mere diversionary ploy to be ignored or deflected unemotionally.

Attaching conditions to concessions

This is a key tactic in effective negotiation. Compromise and concession are, of course, essential aspects of negotiation – otherwise no bargaining can occur – but every effort should be taken to minimise the loss of benefit involved. This is partly just a matter of hard bargaining against the background of the two parties' relative power. Against a union claim for a 9 per cent wage increase, 6½ per cent may be a reasonable settlement if the union's case and its ability to apply sanctions is weak; 8 per cent may be a good settlement if the reverse is true. But another approach is to introduce a condition to the settlement – something for something rather than something for nothing.

How is this best done? The golden rules are:

- Introduce the condition before talking about the concession.
- Do not give details of the concession until there is an indication that the condition is negotiable.

If the possibility of a concession is raised before the condition, the other party will seize on it as an offer and it will then be difficult to say that it is conditional. To give details of what the concession might be before the other side has shown any willingness to consider the condition runs similar risks. Two industrial relations cases illustrate the point:

A trade union had submitted a claim for a shorter working week and longer annual leave. The company was ready to make some movement on total working time but did not want to alter current patterns of shift work, so the management response, put briefly, was: 'If you are prepared to set aside this year's claim for a shorter working week, we might be able to talk about annual leave.' The condition – dropping the working week claim – was put first, so any concession would clearly be conditional. No details of the possible concession were given, pending an indication by the union that they were prepared to consider the condition.

A union was claiming a 5 per cent wage rise, the management had offered 3 per cent but were under great pressure to go further. The line they then took was: 'If we were to consider any higher we would have to bring forward a proposal we had originally intended to put to you later in the year – the need to introduce a Saturday shift on plain time instead of overtime rates.' So any concession on wages (unspecified at this stage) would clearly be conditional on agreement about a wholly new issue.

The use of emotion

A general rule in negotiating is to avoid becoming emotionally committed. It is difficult to exercise the necessary imagination and flexibility if one has developed a strong personal or emotional commitment to a fixed point of view. As already noted, it is also dangerous to rise to the bait of personal attack. It is the issues that should be concentrated on, not the defence of personal dignity or the scoring of debating points.

There are occasions, however, when a controlled display of emotion may be beneficial. The two conditions are that the emotion *must* be sincere, and its use should be a *conscious* decision, not an instant reaction. Two examples follow:

A negotiation about a supply contract between the managerial teams of two firms had degenerated into little better than a slanging match on points of detail. This was brought to an end by one older manager, much respected in the industry, interrupting the argument with an obviously deeply-felt plea that all concerned should set personal differences aside, respect one another's professional competence, and concentrate on finding a solution to the business problem involved.

A national trade union leader swayed the employers' attitudes in a wage-bargaining session by a very sincere and strongly-felt plea that some improvement should be made to wage rates for the lowest paid categories – mainly women working part-time in cleaning and catering. He admitted that in strict market or supply and demand terms, his case was weak. But by quoting actual cases of real hardship, and appealing to the employers' sense of fairness and human sympathy, he created an emotional mood in which the employers found it very difficult to do other than respond favourably.

Key points

- One's own negotiating position can be strengthened by identifying and tactfully reminding the other party of sanctions that are available if negotiations fail.
- Sanctions may be financial, legal, or emotional or may relate to the effect of a particular outcome on an organisation's or individual's reputation, image, or self-regard.
- New issues may be introduced into a negotiation as a diversion, or to provide opportunities for trade-offs between parts of a bargaining package.
- Whenever possible, conditions should be attached to concessions – something for something rather than something for nothing.
- When considering concessions, introduce the condition first and do not give details of the concession until the other party shows some willingness to negotiate on the condition.
- Normally, avoid emotional commitment, but displays of emotion may occasionally be beneficial, provided that they are sincere and are used consciously.

9

Timing and Adjournments

People with no negotiating experience sometimes express surprise at how long negotiations can take. 'What on earth can they be talking about all that time?' is a comment often made about nationally publicised negotiations such as the annual EU farm price sessions, or a long series of lengthy meetings at ACAS to resolve an industrial dispute. There are several reasons for this tendency to go on talking rather than moving briskly towards an agreement – and the trend is one that applies to all negotiations, however informal.

- Unlike a formal business meeting with a detailed agenda and an average of perhaps 10 minutes for each item, negotiations often involve a joint exploration of the subject matter and a careful sounding-out of alternatives and possible compromise. The two sides start from different viewpoints, and need time to test and explain their differing perceptions and objectives. In the search for a mutually satisfactory solution each is cautious about conceding too much, too quickly. It is not possible to handle this process of probing, floating ideas and compromise on a very structured basis; the process is organic rather than mechanistic – and that takes time.
- That said, there is sometimes a tendency to assume that the negotiations will be lengthy and, therefore, to set neither a time-scale nor a target completion time or date.
- Knowing that concessions will have to be made, some negotiators are concerned to demonstrate that these are not made lightly. An agreement concluded in half an hour may, they feel, give an impression that they have not fought hard enough for their side's objectives. Only after a very lengthy period of hard argument and bargaining do they feel able to modify their opening position. This is particularly the case when the negotiating team has to report back to their principals – the board of direc-

tors, say, for a management team, or a mass meeting of union members for trade union officials.

Despite these trends, there are some aspects of time that have a major impact on the effectiveness of negotiations, and the effective negotiator will be continuously aware of the changes of mood and attention that the passage of time can bring. The two main points to consider are the duration of each negotiating session and the use of adjournments.

The duration of sessions

When you are planning a negotiation, some thought should be given to the time-scale and an attempt made to strike a balance between an open-ended arrangement – which encourages unduly lengthy talks – and providing too little time for a constructive discussion.

The party taking the initiative in calling the meeting has an advantage here. They can suggest how much time to set aside, or can announce when the meeting starts that, for example, 'We have another appointment later this morning, so we need to aim to finish by 11am.' If it is obvious from the start that the matter is complex and will require more than one meeting, then dates and times can be set at the opening session. There is no doubt that having a target finishing-time – provided that it is realistic – does help to create a positive attitude and a feeling that progress towards a conclusion is being made.

There is evidence, too, that the maximum time for which it is possible to maintain a high degree of continuous attention and positive involvement is little over two hours. Two hours is a reasonable period to set aside for a single, relatively straightforward negotiation; or to spend in one uninterrupted session during a longer bargaining episode.

There is a time factor, too, in the presentation of cases and arguments. If it is thought necessary to open proceedings by making a prepared presentation – as might be the case with a catering contractor's team bidding to secure a service contract – 15 to 20 minutes is probably the longest period to ensure the other party's full interest and attention; and this period should be announced by the presenter's saying, 'We'd like to start by telling you about our service, and we've prepared a 15-minute presentation which we hope you will find interesting.' This prior statement about the time helps to prevent the other party's attention wandering, and reassures them that they will not have to sit through an interminable talk.

At the more informal level, the longest period one person is likely to hold attention during the to and fro of a discussion is as short as two to three minutes. To go beyond that runs the risk of irritating the other side by appearing to want to dominate the discussion or to prevent them from responding effectively. In summary:

- The longest period for effective continuous negotiation is about two hours.
- The optimum time for a prepared presentation is 15 to 20 minutes.
- The longest time for an individual contribution to a discussion is two to three minutes.

The fact that major set-piece negotiations often do not accord with these guidelines is more a matter of logistics than tactics. Top-level negotiators with extremely full diaries assemble from all over the country on a fixed date, many with equally important appointments the following day. There is then a mutual desire to complete the business on the appointed day to avoid disrupting the next day's arrangements. When negotiating difficulties then arise, the only solution is to go on bargaining into the night hours – well past the point at which it is possible for most people to maintain an alert and balanced approach. Bargaining to exhaustion has its place in the annals of negotiation but cannot be recommended as a normal or effective tactic.

Adjournments

It follows on from the two-hour rule that in a bargaining session which needs to run for a longer period breaks or adjournments should be taken at around the two-hour mark. Normally, these can be timed to coincide with a refreshment break.

Adjournments may, though, be suggested at any time and there are at least three other constructive uses of the *ad hoc* (as distinct from scheduled) break:

- to give the parties an opportunity to withdraw and review progress among themselves or consider a proposal put by the other side. There is no need to respond immediately or intuitively to such a proposal. Just say: 'That's an interesting new point, which we need time to consider. I suggest we all break for 20 minutes so that our side can talk it over among ourselves.'
- to provide a break if the negotiations have reached an impasse or become bogged down in trivia or personal argument. Again, it is just a matter of taking the initiative in making a suggestion like 'I think it might be helpful if we had a short break at this point so that we can each consider where the discussion is going.' It is surprising how much the atmosphere of a negotiation can improve after a short interruption of this kind.
- to provide an opportunity for one or two members of each side to talk informally with each other away from the bargaining table. It may be possible to explore ways forward in a very informal manner that would not be appropriate in the formal bargaining arena. So the leader of one side, sensing that the moment is right for such a suggestion, might say to his or her opposite number: 'Do you agree that it might be helpful if we adjourn for half an hour while you and I consider, without formal commitment, whether progress might be made by a different approach?' It is not possible, of course, to insist on such an arrangement – but the negotiator on the other side may well agree that it is worth trying. The comment about 'no commitment' is made to reassure the others in the two teams that their leaders will not strike any formal deal without prior reference back.

The effective use of adjournments of the three kinds just outlined is a very important skill to acquire. Any experienced negotiator can quote numerous examples of negotiations that succeeded primarily because adjournments were used to stop unconstructive argument or to open the door to informal soundings between leaders from which eventual solutions have emerged.

Inexperienced negotiators should also pay particular attention to the value of an adjournment to create time to consider unexpected developments. There is never an excuse for being 'bounced' into an unsatisfactory agreement. One party cannot prevent the other from taking time out to review their position and, if such time is needed, an adjournment is the way to secure it.

Key points

- In planning and conducting negotiations, positive attention should be paid to the duration of bargaining sessions, formal presentations, and individual contributions to the discussion.
- A continuous session should rarely exceed two hours, a formal presentation 15 to 20 minutes, and an informal contribution two to three minutes.
- Adjournments coincident with refreshments should be used to break a lengthy negotiation into two-hour segments.
- Adjournments should be used as powerful aids to negotiation by:
  - providing time to consider progress or new proposals within the team and avoid snap decisions
  - bringing unconstructive or personalised arguments to an end
  - providing an opportunity for informal, exploratory talks between individual members of the two parties.

10
Searching for Common Ground

Inexperienced negotiators tend to overconcentrate on the adversarial aspects of negotiation – defending their own opening positions and trying to expose flaws in the other party's case. There is a role for these aspects, particularly if the other party adopts an aggressive stance, but they should not dominate or set the tone of the negotiations if this can be avoided. It should always be kept in mind that the purpose of a negotiation is *to reach an agreement*, not to demonstrate one's own virtues or to score points off the opposition. An agreement is by definition an outcome in which both parties see some advantage. Negotiating towards agreement means moving from different positions towards common ground.

This constructive approach is particularly, though by no means exclusively, relevant to negotiation between managers. Underlying the substance of daily managerial relationships within any organisation there is – or should be – a common concern for the well-being of the organisation as a whole. Managers often become involved in heated arguments about the merits of conflicting ideas or proposals. Too often, defending one's own view (in reality, defending personal pride or prestige) can become the objective of the argument. The wise manager will depersonalise such arguments by standing back from the disputed detail and encouraging those involved to examine the issue from a corporate, organisational viewpoint. Which of the disputed ideas will best serve the interests of the company? Which best fits the organisation's values or style?

As well as a general emphasis on the need to search for common ground, this chapter looks at several ways of reducing tension and disagreement and identifying the shared interests on which an agreement may eventually be constructed:

- listening and asking questions
- the use of humour
- reading between the lines – looking for 'coded' signals
- looking for links between the two cases.

Listening

One of the most common negotiating faults is saying too much and listening too little. Of course, in the opening phase of a negotiation it is necessary to state one's position and make an initial response to the case made by the other party. But once both parties' positions are clear, the discussion needs to move into a more collaborative or exploratory phase in which the search is on for common ground and a mutually acceptable outcome. In this phase, acute attention needs to be given to what the other side are saying and how they say it. What are their real concerns? How might they react to a possible way forward? Are they beginning to shift their ground? The answers will be found by perceptive listening, not by continuing to talk.

It may be thought that if the other party also adopts a listening posture, the discussion will dry up. To prevent this, the tactic is to switch from making statements or rebutting arguments to asking questions – and listening intently to the tone, as well as the substance, of the answers.

Aileen Kenney was the marketing manager of a low-cost furniture manufacturer. The production director was John Steel, a no-nonsense, efficiency-minded manager with little time for the niceties of public relations. There had recently been some very adverse publicity about the fire risks of the company's products in the local press, following two child deaths in a house fire. The regional television station had just telephoned John, asking for him to be interviewed on the subject. He had refused, telling the reporter he had nothing to say but that they might contact the marketing manager. He told Aileen he had said this. She went to see him to discuss what the company response should be.

Initially, the discussion was extremely sticky. 'Tell them what you like,' said John, 'provided that you don't commit me to doing anything.' Aileen was very unhappy with this. She pointed out that this put her in an impossible position if she was to project the

69

company in a favourable light. She wanted to say that there was a current problem with the availability of flame-proofed materials but that the company, while in no different position from most others in the industry, had plans well in hand for new, improved product ranges. She argued, too, that the story was likely to be given to the national press if the company upset the local media. 'That's not my worry,' was John's reply.

Aileen then switched to a questioning approach. 'Forget the present case for the moment,' she suggested. 'What is the general trend in the use of new materials in the industry over the next five years?' John began to talk technicalities, which she encouraged. 'How many weeks' stock have we got of the old materials?' she asked. 'Are there significant production problems in a phased introduction of the new materials?' She went on: 'If I felt we could live with a price increase of 5 per cent, would that cover any increased material costs?'

By the questioning process, it eventually became apparent that John's intransigence about the television interview was not based on a cool, analytical assessment of the situation, looked at from a company viewpoint, but a resentful reaction to what he had felt was implied personal criticism. By drawing this out, and then asking John for interesting information about new production plans, she was able to agree a very positive line to take in the television interview. Questions, rather than statements, were the key to her success, linked to an emphasis on what was good for the company.

The use of humour

Negotiations are serious matters, and there is no place for flippancy. Humour and the occasional light-hearted remark can be used, however, to relieve tension and contribute to establishing a shared, rather than confrontational relationship.

It is interesting to observe the first few minutes' interaction between two experienced, old-style negotiators – either as individuals or teams. Almost inevitably, there is a short period of good-natured banter. 'Open the windows,' the leader of one party will say, 'George has brought his fumigator!' – referring to the other leader's pipe. To which George will respond: 'I brought it to kill the bugs in your office!' Why has this sort of ritual been seen as both normal and useful? It serves two functions: helping to reduce the underlying tension, and encouraging a joint, rather than confrontational, mode. This bonding is not particularly strong. It can easily break down under the later pressure of serious disagreement. But many negotiations make better progress if the initial ritual *bonhomie* is reinforced from time to time during the discussions by a well-timed, light-hearted or humorous comment. This is not a matter of interrupting the discussion to tell irrelevant jokes, nor does it call for any great wit. Indeed, the too-clever remark may be seen as sarcasm rather than humour. Instead it usually involves spotting the occasional absurdity or mistake (if possible in what one's own side have said) and drawing attention to its funny side. Its implication must be that we are all in this together, we are all human and fallible, and so let us all keep a sense of proportion. It is, unfortunately, impossible to define in terms of a formula or set of principles – but it should not be overlooked. As was implied in the section about negotiating style in Chapter 5, care must also be taken to avoid 'funny' remarks that some negotiators might perceive as rude, patronising, or discriminatory.

Reading between the lines

Experienced negotiators are very wary of committing themselves to definite statements until they are confident that this will not prejudice their position. Their initial moves will be hedged about with reservations, or couched in indeterminate form so that they can quickly withdraw before the other party can seize on a statement as a specific concession. When the negotiation is in its exploratory phase it is, consequently, of great importance that every hint of a change of position or a possible way forward is picked up.

There is a whole vocabulary of such 'coded' messages or signals. A few of the more common, together with their interpretations, are:

- 'There is no possibility of our going that far at this stage.' But there may be a possibility of movement later.
- 'It would not be our normal business practice to do that.' But if the price was right, we might make an exception.

71

- 'You have put these proposals in a form which we find unacceptable.' But if they were repackaged, some progress might be possible.
- 'What we must make clear is that points (a) and (b) are totally unacceptable.' But points (c) and (d) are worth talking about.
- 'We can certainly agree on the basic principles.' But there are still major problems with the actual details.

Hints and signals are not always verbal. They may be identified from changes in tone, facial expression or posture. A note of hesitation or embarrassment may creep in if the speaker has no conviction in what is being said. A combative pose – arms folded or hands clenched – may be changed to a more open or relaxed position. Leaning forward generally indicates interest. Face-touching is often connected with doubt or uncertainty. Eyebrow-raising is a classic indication of surprise. Glances between the members of a negotiating team can indicate when significant points have been made. Most indications of this kind are unconscious but some gestures can be used intentionally. For example, one way of emphasising the finality of a statement is to accompany it with a firm gesture of the hand – placing it palm down on the table. The interpretation of body language needs to be used with caution – it is not an exact science. But to overlook the signals that can be read from posture, gesture, and facial expression is to miss a potentially rich source of indications of attitude and intention. Looking for and understanding the signals carried by body language can help the effective negotiator interpret the real meanings that may be hidden behind the actual words being used. There may also be a change of spokesperson within the team, with an assertive speaker making way for someone who has been listening quietly up to this point.

Looking for links

Both parties to a negotiation share at least two objectives. One is the general wish, whatever the subject, to reach a satisfactory outcome, preferably without unpleasantness or overlengthy time involvement. The other, specific to each case, is that the agreement should have some benefit or advantage.

The first can be used to encourage the other party to co-operate in maintaining a reasonably brisk, business-like pace and equable atmosphere to the negotiation. If the discussion becomes bogged down in trivia, repetition, or personal acrimony an appeal can be made to the parties' joint interest in making progress and avoiding time-wasting. As the leader in one negotiation put it: 'I am sure neither side wants to spend their valuable time picking over the bones – wouldn't it be better if we set aside our current argument and concentrated on the main point at issue.'

The second point – that the parties share an interest in a favourable outcome – may not be quite so obvious. Each side's interpretation of 'favourable' will be different. Yet ultimately they will have to take joint responsibility for an agreement – and each needs to be able to consider this to be at least acceptable before they can be expected to endorse it. The link between them is the common action or outcome which they do eventually agree, and their joint need to consider this outcome justified.

The advantage may, of course, be somewhat one-sided. An employer may agree a high wage settlement fairly grudgingly, with all the perceived advantage going to the trade union. Yet even here, there are links between the parties that will help the employer come to terms with the outcome. Directly, the settlement will remove the sanction of industrial action. More constructively, it will help the employer achieve or improve the organisation's recruitment and retention capability.

In working towards an agreement it is, consequently, helpful to consider not just the pros and cons of alternative outcomes to one's own side but to think also of what common interest exists, and what benefits each alternative has for the other side.

In a factory dispute, the trade union was demanding the dismissal of a foreman for alleged racial abuse towards a black employee. The company felt it had to resist this because it was the first time any complaint of this kind had been made against the foreman, and because he was in all other respects one of their most experienced and competent supervisors. So the opening positions of the two sides were diametrically opposed – dismissal or no dismissal.

The eventual agreed solution was a warning to the foreman, an apology to the employee, and the introduction of an equal opportunity training programme for all supervisory staff. The link between the two sides that led to this outcome was that both were concerned to ensure that no such incident occurred again. The training programme was seen by both parties as being a far more constructive way of achieving this than the dismissal that the union had originally sought.

A concentration on common interests, instead of on the original differences, is a key to effective negotiation. If the possible solution to an apparently narrow and hotly disputed issue can be shown to contribute to the achievement of broader objectives, breaking a deadlock and reaching agreement are often made easier. These common interests often include:

- company success and business prosperity
- job security
- company reputation – both commercially and as a good employer
- avoidance of wastage or environmental damage
- individual reputation – for professionalism, integrity, skill
- an image of being constructive as a negotiator
- maintenance of high morale
- avoiding interference by third parties.

Key points

- The purpose of negotiation is to reach agreement, not to score points in argument.
- Effective negotiators are good listeners: they ask questions more often than they make statements.
- Humour, or good-natured banter, can be used to reduce tension and help create a bond between the two parties.
- It is important to look for verbal and non-verbal clues or signals of the other party's changes of mood or approach.
- There should be a concentration on issues or outcomes of common interest, rather than on the original differences.

11
Working towards Agreement

There comes a point in all negotiations when the discussion needs to move from an exploration of the issues and a careful sounding out by each party of the other's possibly changing position towards a positive consideration of specific proposals for agreement. Handling this phase well is crucial. One bad or tactless move and the other side's willingness to reach agreement may be lost. Several aspects of this phase need to be considered:

- the use of periodic summaries
- using hypothetical suggestions
- helping the other party to move
- avoiding loss of face
- constructive compromise.

Periodic summaries

In a negotiation in which a number of issues are involved it is not unusual for progress to be made faster on some matters than others. Unless this is defined and accepted as it occurs, there is a danger that a later disagreement on another issue may lead to back-tracking and the loss of earlier progress.

It is helpful, therefore, to pause from time to time to summarise where the discussion has led and thus secure a step-by-step movement towards eventual full agreement. The negotiation about working time, quoted in several previous examples, can be used to illustrate this:

> The discussion had reached the point at which it had become clear that levels of overtime were a key issue that now needed discussion. At this point, the management side's leader said: 'Before

we go on to talk about overtime, I think we might all find it helpful to summarise where we have got to so far. The company has explained why it cannot consider a reduction in the working week. But we have accepted that some movement should be made on annual leave, and our proposition – which I take it you have agreed with, at least in principle – is that the manual employees' entitlement should be harmonised with that of the clerical staff. Is everyone happy with that summary? If so, we'll just make a quick note of it so that we don't waste time later trying to remember what we said.'

The effect of this summary was to lock both parties in to an agreed approach to the annual leave issue, and prevent a possible dispute on overtime upsetting the progress that had already been made.

A summary may, of course, reveal that the two sides have different understandings about the position that has been reached. This may be frustrating – but it provides a useful opportunity to clear up any differences during the negotiation. However, it is even more frustrating when people believe that a final agreement has been reached, only to discover differences of understanding about a point that both parties had assumed was settled earlier.

Hypothetical suggestions

The introduction of specific proposals after a period of cautious exploration of the issues is sometimes a difficult transition to handle. One way of easing into it is initially to float the proposals as hypothetical or on a no-commitment basis. This enables the other party to present their initial reactions as similarly provisional, and one's own side to withdraw without losing bargaining flexibility.

Jenny Sadler, a local authority finance manager, was trying to persuade Ronald Gower, the housing manager, to accept a new method of costing maintenance work. He was wedded to his present system, which was proving difficult to computerise, although it gave him the information he needed for day-to-day purposes, it involved too much manual processing time in the finance department. At an earlier meeting, Jenny had presented him with a fully worked-out and completely new system that he rejected out of hand as being designed solely to help the accountants. This time she changed her tactics.

'Looking at it from your point of view,' she said, 'what might your reaction be if it was possible to simplify the daily worksheets that your supervisors have to complete? I'm not sure how far we could take this, but if you are willing to consider it, without commitment at this stage, I could work up something specific.' George agreed that this was worth taking further, and Jenny was able to go on to another element in her plan, selling this on a similar basis of the benefits in it to George, and the absence of pressure on him to give an immediate, and final, yes or no.

Floating ideas in this way gets proposals on to the table without creating a strong commitment by one party to defend them, or the other to oppose. A more relaxed discussion can ensue, with adjustments to the original idea arising jointly, rather than being perceived as victories or defeats. Some typical phrases used in introducing proposals in this way are:

- 'Just for the sake of argument, what might your views be if we suggested that . . .?'
- 'Without pressing you for a formal response, what would your feeling be about . . .?'
- 'Suppose we thought of doing something along these lines – how might you react?'
- 'We had thought that we might suggest x, but we are not sure that this is quite what you had in mind.'
- 'Have you thought about y? It is something we might find possible to consider.'

Helping the other party to move

Two very human tendencies can inhibit progress in the closing stages of negotiation:

- a reluctance to be seen to be modifying one's original position
- a temptation to gloat over any retreat by the other party.

These tendencies are exacerbated by viewing negotiation in terms of winning and losing, rather than as a process of reaching a jointly satisfactory outcome. One of the most important ways of achieving such an outcome is to make it as easy as possible for the other side to shift their position and agree to compromise – rather than making them feel that they are on the losing side. This may mean going beyond the search for common ground discussed in Chapter 10 and emphasising the particular and different benefits that a proposed outcome offers to the other party. Consider the case of a company negotiating with its trade unions about the introduction of a cashless pay system:

> The company's objective was primarily to introduce a much less costly system of wage payments – in effect, to save money on pay administration. Their real case was that the current cash payment system was out-dated and expensive. But to expect the trade union to agree to a change simply to help the company financially was unrealistic. To help the trade union move towards acceptance of a change, the company needed to identify and explain the benefits to union members. These were described in terms of the advantages of operating bank accounts (a deal had been done with a local bank branch to offer incentives for employees opening accounts) and the elimination of the risk of employees' becoming injured in a wages raid.
> The company's aim was to provide the union officials with a case that could be sold to union members as advantageous to them.

Another tactic is to respond positively rather than critically to any advance, however small, offered by the other side. If, after hours of tedious argument, the other side suggests a minor concession, the temptation may be to reply: 'We could have saved a lot of time if you had agreed to that in the first place instead of wasting two hours defending the indefensible!' Better by far to bite one's tongue and say instead: 'That's a very interesting and responsible suggestion. I am sure it provides a basis for making some real progress.'

Helping the other party to move involves:

- helping them to identify the benefits to their side
- playing down the benefits to one's own side
- encouraging every positive move they make, however small
- applauding the other party's wisdom and helpfulness in making positive movement

78

- avoiding any implication that by moving, they are losing and one's own party is winning.

Saving face

Lying behind much of the reluctance to accept a compromise is loss of face – the fear of apparent personal failure, openly exposed. It is as important to recognise this as a potentially inhibiting factor in oneself as it is to avoid acting in a way that exacerbates the fear in the other party.

Fear of loss of face can be an inhibiting factor in two ways. It may prevent good ideas from emerging within one's own team; it may also work against the making of constructive proposals to or from the other party.

A management team was negotiating an office rent review with a team from the property company who owned their HQ building. The first meeting ended in deadlock and a further meeting had to be scheduled. The management leader called a pre-meeting of his own side for a post-mortem on what had happened and to plan for the next negotiation. One of his team members then said that he had thought that an offer to consider a full repairing lease (under the current lease, the property company was responsible for repairs) might have broken the deadlock. 'Why didn't you suggest that at the time?' asked the management leader. The reply was: 'I didn't want to be the first one to make a concession.'

The person involved had been more concerned with his reputation within his own team as a tough negotiator than with making progress in the negotiations. The ironic feature of these negotiations was that when the two teams next met, the property company started by suggesting that a lower rental might be acceptable if a full repairing lease was introduced – and a mutually satisfactory deal was soon concluded. Asked informally sometime later why the property firm had not suggested this solution at the first meeting, their leader said: 'We didn't want to be the first to make a concession.'

Personal and corporate pride (which is the basis of 'face') had prevented progress both within and between the teams in this example. There is a related point. Loss of face can occur when either party gets itself boxed into a position from which the only escape appears to be a humiliating retreat. An example might be when a negotiator makes an unequivocal statement such as 'This is our absolutely final offer and under no circumstances can we make any further concessions' – only to be confronted with a further and unexpected argument (or demonstration of strength) by the other party which can only be dealt with by a further compromise. The danger is that instead of accepting the humiliation of having to admit that the final offer is not final, negotiations will be broken off and resort had to a more confrontational method of proceeding.

The three things follow from this:

- Unless you are very sure of your position, do not adopt a stance from which movement will be perceived as defeat: always leave a back-door open for a more dignified withdrawal.
- At the same time, do not be thin-skinned about the comment that the other party may make about changes of position. Do not allow considerations of face to get in the way of sensible compromise.
- If necessary, help the other party to keep their back-door open, so that they are not provoked into aggression or confrontation by feeling trapped.

Constructive compromise

There is more than window-dressing or manipulation in seeking to show that a proposed solution has advantages to both parties. The achievement of genuinely constructive compromise involves the widest possible view being taken of what beneficial elements can be included in the agreement. It also involves consideration of wider issues, such as the effect of the negotiations on the quality of the longer-term relationship between the two parties. For example, a company will not want to damage an otherwise excellent commercial relationship with a key supplier by a dispute over a short-term delivery problem; and in industrial relations, it has always to be remembered that company and trade union have to continue their co-existence after each negotiation.

Compromise is often thought of as negative. But if it avoids costly confrontation and secures an effective agreement in which both parties can share a sense of satisfaction and achievement, compromise is both positive and constructive. So in moving towards the conclusion of a negotiation, thought needs to be given to how the advantages in the final agreement can be optimised. Questions that assist this process are:

● Can this or that proposal be used to achieve a wider benefit than first seems possible?
● Can a new condition be introduced to offset the disadvantages of a pending concession?
● Would a change of emphasis or priority secure long-term advantage against short-term loss?
● Might a tactical retreat now on a narrow issue provide a better basis for beginning negotiations on another issue later?
● Can agreement on an apparently minor issue create a useful precedent for use at some later stage?
● Can the negotiation and its outcome be used to create or improve a favourable, more general, relationship with the other party?

It is on questions of this kind that thought needs to be concentrated, rather than worrying about the possibility of every minor compromise being perceived as weakness.

Key points

● The closer a negotiation is to agreement, the more sensitively the discussion should be handled.
● Periodic, jointly agreed summaries of progress can secure a phased agreement and prevent reversion to earlier argument.
● Proposals may initially be put as hypothetical suggestions. This makes it easier for both parties to avoid the pressure of immediate acceptance or withdrawal.
● There is a positive advantage in making it easy for the other side to move, rather than challenging them on a win/lose basis.
● Proposals are best sold on their advantages to the other party, not to one's own.
● Fear of losing personal or corporate face can severely inhibit progress.
● Compromise should be seen as constructive, not weakness.
● In assessing the benefits of an agreement, consideration should be given to factors beyond the context of the immediate negotiation – such as the creation of useful precedents, and the quality of long-term relationships.

12

Clinching Agreement

The final stage in any successful negotiation is the conclusion of an agreement. Even in very informal managerial discussions, an agreed outcome is sought; otherwise there has been no more than a non-productive exchange of views. At the other extreme, in formal commercial bargaining, the outcome is an agreement that will carry legal weight as an enforceable contract.

Securing an effective agreement is aided by paying attention to four aspects:

- closing the deal – timing and credibility
- ensuring all points have been included
- ensuring full understanding – summaries and documentation
- avoiding fudging the issues merely to secure an agreement.

Closing the deal

It is critical in a negotiation to judge when the time has come to bring the exploratory and concession-making stages to an end, to indicate that one can go no further, and to suggest that an agreement be concluded on the basis of the positions reached by that time. Two factors are important: timing, and the credibility of the final position.

It is in the nature of negotiation that the mood or emotional atmosphere of a meeting fluctuates between highs and lows. At one point, things will be going well with a feeling of co-operation and *bonhomie*; then the mood changes as a serious disagreement arises. It is fairly obvious that the right time to bring the negotiation to a successful conclusion is during a high – or at least not during, or in the immediate aftermath of, a bad patch. An adjournment can be used to close the door on an unsatisfactory episode and enable a fresh start to be made – perhaps of the final session.

It is sometimes less easy to convince the other party that no further concessions or compromise are possible; that one has reached the end of the road; and that decisions must now be reached as to whether to settle, or close the negotiation without agreement. This is particularly difficult if you have made a series of minor concessions or revised offers during a lengthy bargaining process, and have unwisely described an earlier position as being 'the last offer'. The other party will have learnt from this that your 'last' may not mean final – how are they to know that you have, in reality, reached your sticking-point?

Statements about finality can, however, be re-inforced in several ways:

- tone of voice and choice of words: a clear, firm, confidently expressed, unapologetic statement that 'We've moved quite a way during this meeting and have taken full account of everything you have put to us. We are now at the point where you must decide whether or not to accept what we have just proposed. It's our absolute limit.'
- change of style: from a discursive mode to a short, crisp statement.
- non-verbal behaviour: such as gathering up all one's papers and putting them in a document case.
- change of format: from purely oral proposals to the tabling of a written final offer – even if this is no more than a quickly hand-written note, passed across the table.

Even when the timing is right and the credibility of the final offer has been established, it may still be necessary to add something to tip the balance in favour of an acceptance. Among the aids to breaking any last-minute deadlock are:

- tying the agreement to some future benefit: 'If we can settle on the terms we have just proposed, we would be willing to re-open discussions on x not later than the end of next year.'
- agreeing that a disputed point can be subject to review: 'We understand why you are reluctant to accept x, and we would be willing to include a review of its effect in 12 months' time.'
- explaining fully why no further concessions are possible, perhaps by bringing in a new member of the management team to

add weight to the case: for example, the sales director might be asked to join the meeting to explain the difficult trends in the overseas market.

● pointing out the adverse consequences of a failure to reach agreement – not in a threatening way but as a cold recitation of fact: 'Much as we wish to avoid it, a failure to agree at this stage would force us to consider legal action – and our lawyers tell us that we should then plan for a 12-month delay and costs on both sides running at over £50,000.'

Ensuring all points have been included

In the euphoria of reaching agreement on a major issue – a wage award, say, or the price for a new contract – it is not unknown for some subsidiary but still important points to be left unclarified.

A personnel director was negotiating the terms of a service contract with the successful candidate for an appointment to a new senior marketing post. The discussions were difficult and protracted, but agreement was eventually reached and the contract duly signed. One of the points raised by the marketing manager in the course of the discussion was the company's policy about the payment of relocation expenses in the event of the office being moved. At that time, although the possibility had been considered by the board, no immediate move was envisaged, and so the personnel director merely gave an oral assurance that the company would 'deal reasonably with any expenses' that the manager might incur. Nothing about this was included in the service agreement. Two years later, the company relocated its offices and the marketing manager moved his home to avoid lengthy daily travel. He then submitted a claim for £25,000 to cover all the costs of a bridging loan, estate agent's, survey, removal, and legal fees, travelling and subsistence for himself and his wife while house-hunting, and various incidental expenses such as new curtains and carpets. The company refused to pay for more than the estate agency, legal, and removal fees, triggering a bad-tempered dispute in which the marketing manager claimed originally to have been given an assurance by the personnel director that all his costs would be covered. The inclusion of a relocation clause in the contract would have prevented this unfortunate misunderstanding.

Failures to define dates – of implementation, review, or duration – are among the most common omissions. Other faults include a failure to define terms (eg does 'wage' mean basic rate, or basic rate plus allowances; does 'normal working week' include routine overtime?).

Ensuring full understanding

The last point relates closely to the need to ensure not just that everything necessary has been included in the agreement but also that the two parties have a common understanding of its terms and intentions. Orally, it is important for the person taking the lead in the negotiation to make a final summary: 'I think we have now reached agreement on all the issues. My understanding is that what we have agreed to is . . .' – going on to list each point.

Assuming there is oral agreement with this summary, the sooner it is committed to writing the better. In negotiations of any substance, managers and others not directly involved are going to ask the participants about what has been agreed. Oral versions, passed on several times, are liable to considerable distortion and the only remedy is the issue, rapidly, of a definitive and jointly agreed statement.

Even in informal discussions, a quick note is often useful.

A production manager had a short meeting with the toolroom shop steward about the operation of the quality bonus. They agreed a minor change to the system. As soon as the meeting had finished, the manager dictated a note:

'I am writing to confirm the outcome of our discussion this morning. You queried the method of calculating the scrap rate when substandard materials were discovered. I agreed that in future, rejects caused by such material would be discounted in the week in which they occurred instead of, as now, one week in arrears. The new system will start on 1 March.'

Note in this example, too, that a start date has been agreed and documented so that there can be no later misunderstanding.

Not all negotiators recognise the importance of written confirmation. This hands an advantage to the side that does, because they can volunteer to produce it. This is not to suggest that in drafting the note distortions or new points can be introduced. That would risk justifiable criticism for deceit. Nevertheless, the party that drafts the agreement does have the advantage of choosing the precise wording, sequence, and emphasis that it considers is the most satisfactory exposition of what has been agreed. So one's own leader can conclude the negotiation by saying: 'We ought to get this down on paper as quickly as possible – we'll produce a draft tomorrow morning and check it with you by telephone.'

Avoiding 'fudge'

Towards the end of a long, difficult negotiation, when agreement has been half-hearted on some issues and others have not really been grasped, there is a temptation to try to bring matters to a conclusion by agreeing a form of words that glosses over the difficult issues – that is, the awkward points are fudged.

For example, a personnel manager had a difficult meeting with the office trade union representative about a variety of issues concerning working conditions and the use of new technology. Among these issues was the question of alleged overcrowding. After a whole day's (not always constructive) discussion, both sides wanted to close the meeting and go home. Most of the specific points had been agreed, but the overcrowding issue had barely been addressed.

The personnel manager persuaded the union representatives to accept the package statement about the whole negotiation which included this clause: 'In determining a revised office layout, the management will have regard to the union's view that the layout, as originally proposed, was not wholly adequate in terms of floor space.'

What did this mean? The personnel manager saw it as a sop to the union and a way of getting agreement on the other issues without committing the company to anything specific. The union saw it as accepting their very precise floor space allocation claims. This misunderstanding eventually led to the agreement on the other issues coming unstuck, and a further dispute arising.

The risk of fudge is greatest when the negotiators are not the people who will have to put the agreement into practice – national pay negotiators, for example, who agree a loose form of words about overtime that then results in argument about their interpretation at local level. It is a risk, too, that may occur if lawyers for two companies act for their principals and are given too little guidance about the practicalities of implementation.

If the clear spelling-out of an agreement means that one party or another withdraws its accord, the answer is to renegotiate the points of difficulty that have been revealed – not to attempt to gloss over them with an imprecise form of words.

Key points

- The final offer and agreement needs to be timed to coincide with a period of constructive discussion – and not be done during a combative phase.
- It is important to achieve credibility for any statement about an offer's being final – the tone and style of such a statement may be as important as its substance.
- Devices can be used to break a deadlock in reaching agreement – such as promises of future negotiations on a related topic, or making the introduction of a new conditions subject to later review.
- Before finalising an agreement, check that all aspects have been agreed, particularly dates for implementation, review or completion; and definitions of terms.
- Ensure full understanding of what has been agreed through final summaries and by producing written confirmation.
- Unresolved issues should not be 'fudged' by producing vague or ambiguous forms of words in order to achieve apparent agreement.

————— 13 —————
Securing Implementation

Reaching and documenting an agreement is not an end in itself. The purpose of any negotiation is to produce an outcome or action. In simple negotiations, the agreement and the outcome may coincide. Seller and buyer bargain about a price, and immediately agreement is reached, the sale is effected. But in many cases there is a delay between the close of negotiations and the agreed action's taking place. There may be an agreement, too, on what the outcome is to be, but no definition as to who has to do what in order to achieve this. During the period of delay between agreement and action, or because of lack of clarity about implementation, some agreements fail to achieve their intended results. Attention to implementation is therefore crucial if effective negotiation is to be translated into effective action.

Three elements in the process require particular attention:

- including an implementation programme in the agreement
- establishing a joint implementation team
- ensuring adequate information and explanation to those affected by the agreement but not involved in the negotiations.

An agreed implementation programme

In any instance in which implementation of what has been agreed is not either immediate or wholly unambiguous, the last part of the negotiation itself should be devoted to agreeing what has to be done, and by whom, to ensure the agreement is effected.

George Jones, a company personnel manager, was handling a protracted and complex negotiation with a trade union team about new flexible working hours. Agreement was eventually reached that instead of a fixed 39-hour week, the standard requirement would be for employees to work an average of 37 hours weekly, calculated over an eight-week period during which actual hours might vary between 35 and 40, depending on production requirements. Unfortunately, both sides in the negotiation were so keen to conclude a deal after many wearisome hours of argument that the implementation – apart from a start date – was not discussed. A variety of problems then occurred as the managers and shop stewards who had not been involved directly in the negotiations – but who had to operate it on a day-to-day basis – began to place their own and differing interpretations on the agreement. George subsequently had to reconvene the negotiating teams to hammer out these implementation details – only to be met by the trade unions' saying that, in light of the difficulties that had occurred, they now wished to see a further reduction to a 36½-hour average.

If George had included a detailed implementation plan as part of the original agreement it is probable that this attempt to re-negotiate would not have occurred.

The same principle applies even to informal managerial discussions. Too often, an agreement to do something is left hanging in mid-air without any definition of time-scales or action plans. The accountant eventually agrees to revise the production manager's costing system, but neither of them clarifies when this revision is to be completed or whether the action lies wholly with the accountant. Three questions need to be answered about any agreement in which implementation is not coincident or immediate:

- When is action to implement going to be started – and finished?
- What has to be done to achieve implementation?
- Who is to undertake this work?

Joint implementation

In many cases, action should be taken by both parties to an agreement. For example, in the case of the new working hours agreement, management should brief the supervisors, and the union negotiators should brief the shop stewards. To ensure that both groups are given the same information, it may, therefore, be helpful to form a joint implementation team. Another example in a different setting emphasises the value in some circumstances of a joint approach to implementation:

> A local authority wanted to review its senior management salary structure, and decided to seek outside assistance from a firm of management consultants. Three consultants were invited to submit proposals, and one was selected for the review – subject to satisfactory negotiation of a fee and detailed terms of reference.
> Having reached agreement on these issues, the discussion turned to implementation. How was the consultant actually to undertake the review? What action or input would be needed from the authority to help make the review most useful? It was eventually agreed that a joint review team would be the best solution, with one of the authority's personnel staff working with a consultant, both under the project direction of a senior consultant.

Joint implementation teams are also a common feature of major business development programmes in which, after initial negotiation about fees or financial contributions, the parties involved evolve a partnership approach to the management of the agreed project.

Information and explanation

Most industrial relations agreements depend for their success on the actions of possibly thousands of individual managers, supervisors, and trade union representatives – none of whom took part in the actual negotiations. Explaining such agreements fully and clearly to all concerned in their implementation is essential. Even in a small company, a deal struck between the chairman and the local union organiser needs to be explained to the supervisors and staff.

It is in this phase that imprecise wording in the original agreement (the 'fudge' referred to in Chapter 12) can be very damaging. A phrase such as 'The company will take such reasonable steps as are practicable to reduce the risk of vehicle accidents within its premises' will be interpreted in widely different ways by different people – a potent source of dispute as to whether or not the agreement is being honoured.

Too often, information about agreements is limited to the

issue of badly drafted notices, or to word-of-mouth messages which become progressively distorted as they pass down the management chain. Any agreement of substance or complexity that concerns people not involved in the original negotiation merits a carefully designed and executed programme of information and explanation. Another common fault in the industrial relations field is for each side independently to issue its own explanation – and for these explanations to differ. Joint agreement on explanatory information, or the issue of such information on a joint basis, is highly desirable.

Again, several questions should be asked:

- Who needs to know about this agreement if it is to be implemented effectively?
- What do they need to know?
- How is this information best communicated (eg in written form or orally)?
- By whom?
- Within what time-scales?

Key points

- An agreement is not successful until it has been effectively implemented.
- It is often helpful to include an implementation programme as an integral part of a negotiated agreement.
- An implementation programme defines what has to be done, when, and by whom.
- For some agreements, implementation may be best effected by a joint team.
- Those affected by, or required to apply, an agreement (though not themselves involved in the actual negotiation) need adequate information and explanation.
- Such action should be based on defining who needs to know what, how, and by whom this information should be given, by what methods, and to what time-scales.

91

——————— 14 ———————

Handling Breakdown

Negotiations are of course not always successful, and the wise negotiator gives prior thought to what action might be needed if
agreement cannot be achieved. Contingency planning of this kind
is not defeatist. It merely accepts the uncertainties of the bargaining process and ensures that thought is given to the consequences
of breakdown *before*, rather than after, the event.

Reviewing what would happen if the negotiation is unsuccess-
ful may also influence the bargaining tactics and objectives. It
may be realised, for example, that in the event of breakdown, the
other party will probably take legal action and that one's own position at law is relatively weak. In such circumstances, it would be
unwise to set too high a target. Alternatively, the breakdown of
negotiations with, say, a supplier, may mean only that new negotiations will then have to be opened with an alternative source of
supply.

The questions to ask before negotiations begin are therefore (if
agreement cannot be concluded):

- Can the matter be resolved by taking unilateral action?
- Is it feasible to maintain the *status quo* as an alternative to what
  was being pursued in the negotiation?
- Has the other party the power to inflict damage (eg industrial
  action, or commercial veto)?
- Can the other side unilaterally refer the matter to a third party,
  such as the courts or an arbitrator?
- Should arbitration or legal action be considered as an option for
  one's own side?
- If referred to a third party, is the outcome likely to be less
  favourable than one's bottom limit?
- Might third-party assistance in the form of conciliation or mediation be helpful?

The main options are to take unilateral action or to use third-party intervention – which can be of two kinds: conciliation (or media-tion) and arbitration. These are discussed in more detail below.

Unilateral action

Let us revisit a general rule suggested in an earlier chapter: do not negotiate if the outcome can be achieved by direct action. But like most rules, this one has exceptions.

For example, in industrial relations there may be many circum-stances in which an employer has the power to impose changes in working conditions, but on which it is normal to seek agreement with the trade unions. An agreed solution is much more likely to be implemented effectively than one which, by its imposition, generates employee resentment. There are parallel situations in many informal managerial interactions. The finance director may have the authority to require line managers to submit a new type of expenditure return, but may also feel it wiser to negotiate their agreement to the change rather than impose it.

In most instances of this kind, however, the option of exercis-ing ultimate power of authority is one that should be retained. Whether or not to use it has to be a matter of judgement in the par-ticular circumstances. Points to consider are:

- What will be the effect of imposition on the quality of the re-lationship with the other party?
- Has the other party the power and the will to be obstructive, even if not wholly able to prevent implementation of the im-posed solution?
- Will any damage caused by a reaction to imposition be worse than either dropping the matter and retaining the *status quo*, or a reference to third-party intervention?

Third-party intervention

An analysis of the realities of breakdown may indicate that it would be unwise to proceed unilaterally, or that one has no power to do so. It may also be unacceptable or impossible for the pos-ition that existed before the negotiation to continue. In such circumstances, third-party intervention may be a useful option to consider. There are two main forms of third-party involvement, though each has two variants.

Conciliation or mediation

In these forms, the third party does not produce a binding decision but works with the parties in dispute to help them reach agreement. The conciliator ensures that the two parties are not misunderstanding each other, and that they have considered all possible angles. The emphasis is on helping them evolve their *own* agreed solution, not on the production of solutions by the conciliator.

The mediator is expected to go further and, after listening to the two sides, to suggest solutions. Neither party, however, is under a formal obligation to accept the mediator's proposals.

Arbitration or court rulings

Here, the third party (arbitrator or a court or tribunal) considers the arguments of both parties and then produces a binding solution or ruling.

Whether arbitration is an option will depend on whether prior and joint agreement exists about its use; without such agreement (or provision for arbitration being contractual) it is not normally open for one party to impose the use of an arbitrator on the other. Ideally, both parties agree, before negotiation begins, that if they fail to reach agreement the matter will be referred to arbitration and each will abide by the arbitrator's decision.

The position is different where use of the legal system (courts or tribunals) is concerned. Here, it is open for one party to pursue a legal claim whether or not the other wishes the matter to be dealt with in this way. The courts can, of course, be used only to resolve issues lying within the purview of statute or common law, and the most frequent use of the law is to deal with contractual disputes and with claims for damages or compensation.

Different forms of conciliation and arbitration exist in different types of negotiation; these are mentioned in each of the next three chapters. Three short examples are given here to illustrate more generally the situations in which various types of third-party intervention need to be considered as part of negotiating strategy:

Conciliation
William Scott, a factory production superintendent, had agreed to the request of Gerry Wickens, a superintendent of another section, to take on transfer an employee with whom there had been a personality clash. But, after three months, Scott also found the employee difficult to deal with and told Wickens that he would have to take him back. After a long discussion, Wickens refused. Scott knew that he had no authority to insist on the transfer back, but felt, too, that the present position was untenable. Some form of intervention by a third party was his only way forward; he had to decide whether he would seek conciliation through the personnel manager or a ruling (in effect, arbitration) from the factory manager. His choice was influenced by his assessment of the likely outcomes. He thought that the personnel manager would be sympathetic to his position, and knew that she was renowned for her persuasive abilities. The factory manager, on the other hand, might well take the view that, having accepted the employee knowing him to be a difficult case, Scott was stuck with the result and must live with it. So he suggested to Wickens, who agreed, that they should explain the problem to the personnel manager and seek her advice.

Arbitration
Newtown Borough Council had let a contract to a construction company to build a town swimming pool. Shortly after contract completion, but before final payments had been made, the filtration system broke down and the pool's opening had to be delayed for several weeks while remedial work was done. As a result, the council lost considerable income from swimming fees, and decided to claim compensation from the main contractor. The contractor blamed the breakdown on financial constraints imposed by the council which allegedly resulted in a different and cheaper filtration system's being installed than the one that the contractor had considered desirable. Negotiations failed to resolve the dispute. However, the contract provided for a reference of any dispute to arbitration, which was how the matter was finally settled – to the satisfaction of the council. Newtown's negotiating objectives were decided in the light of this enforceable reference to arbitration, and an assessment that the council had a strong case.

The council, consequently, gave very little ground in the preliminary negotiations in order to avoid prejudicing their case at arbitration.

Mediation

Technomag Ltd was a small publishing company. The 10 journalists (but not the rest of the staff) were union members, and it was normal for the chief executive to conclude an annual wage agreement with the journalists. On one occasion, they claimed a 10 per cent increase at a time when the going rate in the industry was just over 5 per cent. Negotiations resulted in the union's lowering their claim to 9 per cent and the company's offering 6 per cent, but no agreement could be reached. The chief executive then said that he was considering imposing a 6 per cent settlement – which he thought the non-union staff would be very pleased with – but was willing to consider using the services of a non-executive director as a mediator. The union agree, and the director was asked to consider the views of both sides and then to suggest what the increase should be. Neither the chief executive nor the union agreed in advance to accept the mediating director's proposals but, in the event, his eventual suggestion of a 7 per cent award was accepted.

Conciliation comes closest to normal negotiation and carries the least risk of matters being taken out of one's control. It does not, however, put the other side under heavy pressure to compromise and may not, therefore, be enough to shift the other party from a heavily entrenched position.

Mediation places the parties under much stronger psychological pressure – if short of enforcement – to accept a solution that may be significantly worse than the bottom line.

In arbitration, both parties give up control of the outcome; the risk therefore exists of having a position imposed that hitherto has been considered unacceptable. A very thorough and realistic assessment of the validity of one's own position and arguments is therefore essential before either agreeing to arbitration or allowing negotiations to reach an impasse from which enforceable arbitration or legal action is the only course open to the other side. A common failing is to be overoptimistic about the validity or strength of one's own case, or to underestimate the other party's position. Assessing the weak points in one's own case is of almost more importance than recognising its strengths.

Key points

- Giving thought to the situation that would occur if the negotiations failed to achieve agreement is an essential part of planning for negotiation.
- It is unwise to allow a negotiation to fail if the probable outcome – whether because of action by the other party or through a third-party intervention – is worse than the position reached when breakdown occurs.
- The main options in handling breakdown are to take unilateral action to enforce an outcome or to seek third-party intervention.
- In considering unilateral action, thought should be given to the effect of such action on future working relationships.
- The least extreme form of third-party assistance is conciliation, in which a conciliator works with the two parties to help them reach agreement.
- A more direct form is mediation, in which both parties agree to consider (but are not bound to accept) a solution suggested by the mediator.
- The most powerful and risky form of third-party resolution is arbitration – where both parties bind themselves in advance to accept the arbitrator's solution – or legal action through the courts or tribunals.
- Making sound decisions about the use of conciliation, mediation, or arbitration depends on thorough and accurate assessments of the strength of each party's case.

15

Negotiating by Letter and Phone

Negotiation is normally thought of as an oral process – a to and fro of discussion, argument, and question and answer between two people or two teams meeting face to face. So far, documentation has been considered in this book only in relation to the confirmation of the final agreement in writing. Direct oral discussion is easily the most common negotiating mode, but there are occasions in which correspondence or the telephone can play a useful part, or may even be used as an alternative to a conventional face-to-face meeting.

Negotiating by correspondence

It is not uncommon for commercial and industrial relations negotiations to begin with an exchange of letters, even if these consist of no more than a request for a meeting and confirmation of its time and place. These letters may, though, be used in an attempt to establish an opening position or to set the tone for later negotiation. They should certainly be considered as an integral element of the whole process and not merely as preliminary administration. This point has long been recognised by solicitors, whose initial letters registering, say, their clients' claims for compensation, may be designed to jolt the recipients into taking the matter seriously, or to undermine their complacency. Trade unions, too, use this technique.

> Alan Dickens, personnel manager of a distribution company, received a letter from Sue Macklin, the union district organiser. It said: 'We are seeking an urgent meeting to discuss the very grave situation that has arisen in the dispatch department owing to management's failure to supply our members with protective

footwear. There has been a blatant breach of safety legislation and of the company's safety agreement. If immediate action is not forthcoming we shall have to consider what action is open to us, such as a report to the Health and Safety Executive.'

This letter was clearly designed to make the company sit up and take notice: to create a tone of urgency and importance. It was much more than merely a written request for a meeting: it was part of the negotiation itself.

The experienced negotiator will recognise a ploy of this kind and make a judgement about the best form of response. Of course, if the urgency in the opening letter is justified, the best move will probably be to agree to a very early meeting. But if it is thought that a tactic is being used to bolster an otherwise weak or unimportant issue, the negotiation might be continued by letter.

In this case, that is what Alan Dickens did. He wrote back, saying: 'We are certainly willing to arrange a meeting should this prove necessary, but to avoid any waste of time it would be helpful if you would first let me have a note of whatever action the dispatch department's shop steward has taken to resolve the matter within the department. Perhaps you could also explain whether your reference to safety shoes refers to the loading bay, as we have no record of any previous discussions about this subject for any other section.'

This letter put the ball back in the union's court. There was a two-week delay until a further letter was received, giving more specific details of the complaint. The delay, and the receipt of the second letter, enabled Dickens to conduct his own investigation and to prepare a constructive response – also by letter – that resolved what was, in fact, a minor matter, without a meeting having to take place.

Although in many instances it would be unwise or unsatisfactory to attempt to conduct negotiations solely by correspondence, there are situations in which such a course may offer some advantages over face-to-face meetings:

● Much time may be saved. Negotiating meetings are notoriously time-consuming, even when minor matters are being considered. In the case just quoted, it is not improbable that a meeting involving perhaps two managers and three trade union officials would have lasted a couple of hours. Producing two or three letters and reading the replies took less than half this time.

- It may be possible to avoid an otherwise emotionally charged meeting and deal with the problem much more rationally. It may be known that a manager or trade union official is an excitable or belligerent negotiator at meetings. Dealing with an issue through correspondence may elicit a more reasonable response.
- The negotiation will be on record – which may be an important point if there is a possibility of eventual legal action.
- If very complex proposals are involved, putting them in writing should help to eliminate the risk of misunderstanding which can sometimes arise in the heat of oral negotiation. Time can be given to the very careful drafting of a written proposal (or response to the other party's position), and this is not subject to the immediate challenge or even interruption which can occur in a meeting.

In practice, a mixture of written and oral negotiation is often the best procedure. The negotiations may start with a short exchange of letters in which both parties clarify their intentions. A meeting (or meetings) then takes place. At this point one party may suggest an adjournment for a few days while they review the position, and follow this with a letter setting out detailed proposals which are then the subject of further direct negotiation. Eventually an agreement is reached, which is confirmed in writing.

Negotiating by telephone

Lengthy or complex negotiations cannot be conducted on the telephone but there are occasions when this mode of negotiation is extremely effective. There is something about the telephone that encourages at least some people to be more co-operative than in face-to-face discussions. The unplanned or unexpected nature of a phone call, which may interrupt higher-priority work, sometimes reduces the care and resistance usually exercised in face-to-face negotiation.

The local manager of a security firm telephoned the administration manager of a client company and asked for a meeting to discuss possible alterations to the detail of the contract for night security services. Instead of fixing a date for a meeting, the administration manager said: 'I have a very heavy diary over the next couple of weeks: have you got a few minutes to talk about it on the phone now?' In the resultant telephone discussion, the security company's proposals were quickly modified and an alternative revision agreed – subject to written confirmation. The security manager later commented, somewhat ruefully, that he should have insisted on a meeting, because he found himself agreeing to the administration manager's counter-proposals far too readily.

Another case illustrates many managers' experience that points of detail which can involve lengthy discussion at a meeting may be agreed very quickly on the telephone:

A company personnel manager had just concluded a very long negotiation with the white-collar trade union about revisions to car allowances. He then realised that both parties had omitted to deal with the small number of staff who were paid a motorcycle allowance. Should he reconvene the meeting? He decided not to. Instead, he phoned the union official and said: 'We need to round off the car allowance agreement by an adjustment to the motorcycle figures. I've checked the latest RAC statistics and an increase of 3p per mile seems justified. Is this OK with you?' To which the answer, after a very short pause for thought, was yes. The personnel manager was relieved at this rapid resolution, because he remembered a lengthy argument about these payments at the previous year's negotiating meeting.

There is a danger, of course, that such attempts at quick deals will misfire: that the answer will be no. Negotiators who try to get quick results by using the telephone should be reasonably confident that their opposite numbers have less skill in the use of this particular mode of bargaining.

Key points

- Face-to-face discussions are not the only form of negotiation: effective use can also be made of correspondence and the telephone.
- An opening letter can help to set the parameters and style of later negotiation.
- Dealing with all or part of a negotiation by correspondence may well save time, avoid an emotional confrontation, provide a record of the negotiation, and enable carefully drafted and complex proposals to be produced.
- Some negotiators are less resistant to proposals when discussing them on the telephone.
- Telephone discussions may be used to settle minor or simple negotiating points extremely quickly.

16

Handling the Media

Newspapers, radio, and television have always been interested in major industrial relations issues – particularly when negotiations break down and strikes occur. Similar interest is shown in some highly publicised commercial battles. In recent years there have been two related developments that have brought more managers into contact with the media than just the heads of major national or international companies:

- A growth in local radio and television has resulted in even quite small-scale negotiations' being covered by news stories and interviews. A dispute about impending redundancies in a local factory or news of the negotiation of the sale of some land for a new hotel are the types of incident that help to make up the daily diet of local journalists.
- To an increasing extent, companies are actively using the media – whether through advertisements or interviews – as a channel of communication to influence the outcome of commercial and industrial relations negotiations. Instead of just responding, often reluctantly, to media requests for statements, they are commissioning public relations and advertising consultants to advise on how the media can be used to promote their negotiating objectives, or to gain public understanding and support.

Negotiations themselves cannot be conducted through the press or television, but in some situations thought should be given to the active use of the media as a channel of communication and influence; and to the response to be given to media requests for news and comment about negotiating issues of public interest.

If a manager becomes involved in media comment, or if it is decided to issue statements or notices to the media, the two main aspects to consider are:

- the characteristics of effective media communication
- the choice of media and the method of communication.

Effective media communication

It should be recognised that in any use of the media, two audiences are involved – the other party to the negotiation or dispute, and the public at large. Public opinion can have a significant effect, particularly on employees during a strike. A feeling that public support has been lost undermines strikers' morale – and the converse is also true. So one aim of media messages is to influence public attitudes.

In doing this, though, it must be remembered that whereas the public may not be able to spot errors or distortions in a story, those directly involved will, and this may well generate an even firmer resolve by the other party to continue their resistance.

There are, then, three main characteristics of effective media communications:

- *accuracy:* facts and figures should be accurate and capable of being proved right if challenged. Although some selectivity or simplification is often necessary, this should not be so blatant as to lead to justifiable charges of distortion and omission.
- *clarity:* however complex or technical the issues, the language (written or spoken) must be simple, direct, and understandable to the lay person.
- *reasonableness:* whatever the provocation, it is desirable to promote an impression of solid common sense and sweet reason – not rancour or rhetoric.

These points are illustrated in the following examples of the use of different media.

The choice of media and method

There are a number of ways of getting one's case into the public domain:

- press advertisements
- press releases
- press conferences
- news stories
- radio or TV interviews.

Press advertisements

There is only one way to retain total control over the wording and presentation of a message and avoid any editorial cutting – to buy advertising space. It is a method that has been used by large employers during industrial disputes, by major companies involved in takeover battles, and by bodies such as the BMA (British Medical Association) wanting to influence their negotiations with government.

If total control is the advantage, then the disadvantage is that the advertisement carries less weight with the public (and perhaps the other party) than news stories or editorial comment. Advertisements are taken with a pinch of salt. Their most effective use is probably to give very straightforward information, rather than views or comment.

In one lengthy local dispute, about 500 factory employees went on strike over plans to introduce new shiftwork schedules. The strike was unofficial, and included a number of employees who – so far as the company knew – were not union members. It was far from clear that communications to the strikers through the union office would be passed on to all those involved, and because of high labour turnover the company was not confident that its records of home addresses were wholly reliable. Yet a point was reached when it was necessary to get a message across to all the employees. A full-page advertisement was, therefore, placed in both the local papers, addressed very specifically to the employees on strike and saying in very unambiguous terms that everyone who reported for work on the following Monday morning would be able to resume work without any detriment to holiday pay, but that anyone not so reporting would be deemed to have resigned.

The wisdom of such an ultimatum might be open to question: what was undisputed was that the message did get across to all concerned. Even those who read neither paper had it quickly drawn to their attention by relatives or friends.

Press releases

A press release is a prepared statement issued to newspapers, radio, and television for them to use or not as they think fit. Like the advertisement, it has the merit of being a statement that is, at least initially, under the control of the initiator – but there the resemblance ends. The media are under no obligation to print the statement as it stands, or at all. It may be ignored, because it is considered unnewsworthy. It may be reproduced in full. Often, however, it will be used merely as the basis for a news story written by journalists who may quote selectively from it. It can be frustrating in the extreme – and may be damaging to one's negotiating interests – to find just one phrase from a carefully prepared statement embedded in a not wholly accurate news story.

To stand the best chance of being used with minimum editorial interference, press releases should be clear, concise, and written in the same style as the media concerned use in their own stories. One idea, often employed successfully, is to personalise the message by giving it as a quote from a named person:

> The first draft of a press release produced by a company production manager about an industrial dispute read:
> 'Messrs AMD Ltd regret to announce that despite their offer to the unions to resolve the current dispute by consolidating attendance allowances within the bonus calculator, thus generating a multiplying effect on the already generous production bonus, it proved impossible at a meeting this morning to persuade the unions to terminate their industrial action.'
> The company's press officer hastily rewrote this as:
> 'Speaking at the end of a long meeting with trade union secretary John Brown this morning, Adrian Green, AMD's production manager, said: 'We're almost at the end of the line in this dispute. We upped the value of our offer from about 5 per cent to a package worth nearly 8 per cent when better bonuses are taken into account, but the union wouldn't budge an inch. They say the strike goes on. We think it's about time they gave their members a chance to say what they think about this much improved offer.'
> This statement was reproduced word for word in the local paper and on local radio. It helped the company's local reputation and played a part in influencing the employees to put pressure on the union officials to call a mass meeting to consider the company's new offer.

Press conferences

On an issue for which maximum publicity is sought – perhaps to generate public opposition to a local authority's planning decision which has been the subject of abortive negotiation – the issue of a press release or official statement can be combined with a press conference. Media journalists are invited to attend, with the lure of a promise of a newsworthy statement followed by a question and answer session.

To ensure good attendance, it is best to fix a venue convenient to the media, such as a town centre hotel. It is also normal to provide light (or liquid) refreshments, and to say so when issuing the invitations to attend.

The advantage of a press conference is that it provides an opportunity to provide much more information and explanation than can be given in a short press release. There are three possible disadvantages or risks:

- No one may attend as a result of other more immediate news items taking editorial priority on the day.
- The questioning may be hostile, or concentrate on issues not central to the case that the company wants to make.
- No control whatsoever can be exercised over the news stories that may be written. Busy journalists or subeditors may limit the story they print to just one item in what was a quite complex statement or discussion; this is likely to be what the media consider newsworthy, and may be peripheral to the company's case.

News stories

A less formal, and often more successful, way of getting the organisation's case into the media is to telephone the relevant news desk, say there is a story to tell, and invite a journalist to listen – either on the phone or by meeting. Any resultant story is likely to be written as a straightforward news item, rather than as an account of a company-initiated news event. It may, therefore, carry more credibility with the readers.

Organisations employing press or public relations officers

ensure that good relationships are cultivated with a few key journalists who can be relied on to listen to a company story and, if they consider it newsworthy, to write it up fairly.

Radio or TV interviews

In other instances, it is the media who initiate contact with the organisation, asking for information or comment. Such approaches can range from an informal telephone call from the local paper, asking for immediate comment, to a pre-arranged interview on radio or TV. All such contacts, however informal, need to be handled with care. The telephone call from a journalist needs particular care. It is by no means uncommon for a manager to treat such a call as a relatively casual matter, with the skilled journalist adopting a very friendly, conversational, rather than interrogative manner. The manager may not realise that what is said may be quoted verbatim, and built up into a major story.

The personnel director of a large local authority was telephoned by the industrial reporter of a national daily and asked for his comments about a government White Paper proposing the extension of compulsory competitive tendering to the personnel function. The reporter gave the impression that it was simply an informal conversation, primarily to help her understand the practical implications of the government's proposals for a typical city council. In the course of the conversation, the personnel director spoke very disparagingly about the motivation of the government minister involved. He was taken aback the next day to see a news story about the White Paper headlined: MINISTER'S PRIVATISATION PLAN SPITEFUL SAYS COUNCIL CHIEF – a breach of the non-political standard of behaviour expected of a senior public servant. In later negotiations about the council's management of competitive tendering, the incident was quoted by a private-sector contractor as evidence of political bias among the management.

The essential requirement, when telephoned by a journalist, is to check the status of the conversation before giving any information or making any comment. 'Are you getting background, or is this discussion for the record?' is the question to ask; and even then be very cautious about saying anything that, if quoted out of context, might damage the organisation's case. (Whether a journalist respects a statement that a conversation is 'off the record' is a matter of judgement – a statement of this kind has no legally binding status.)

More time is available to consider what one wants to say in pre-arranged radio or TV interviews. It is normal, too, before the interview starts, for the interviewer to outline the intended subject matter of his or her questions. But this is to safeguard against the unexpectedly awkward question:

> The manager of a port authority was interviewed on the local TV network about a dock strike. The interviewer explained in advance that he would be asking about the employer's views of the effect of the strike on jobs, and about the action that the employers might have to take to protect their business. However, the manager was visibly disconcerted by the very first question in the interview itself, which was 'When are you going to begin sacking the dockers who are now on strike?'

The key to handling such interviews successfully is to decide in advance on the one or two (no more) important points to be got across, *regardless of what questions are asked.* Good interviewees are not passive respondents who allow the interviewer to control the style and scope of the verbal exchange. A media interview is neither a test of the ability to say as little as possible under interrogation nor an occasion to feed the interviewer with the replies that, from a media viewpoint, make good television. It is an opportunity to communicate one's case to a very wide audience.

The interviewer is, in practice, very unlikely to ask the ideal question from the interviewee's viewpoint. One needs, therefore, to prepare a short, crisp statement encapsulating the most important point to be made, and think how this can be given in response to whatever question might be asked.

> Take the example of Adrian Green of AMD Ltd, referred to earlier in this chapter. Interviewed on local TV after issuing the press statement, he was asked: 'Mr Green, you were not able to settle the strike at your meeting this morning – what are you going to do next?' His reply, prepared in advance as an all-purpose answer to almost any question, was 'The real issue is when is the union going to allow their members to have a say about the company's

109

latest offer?' It was an answer that with very little amendment, could have been given to almost any question he might have been asked, and it concentrated on the message that Green wanted to register both with the public and with his employees.

In this and the other examples given in this chapter, handling the media skilfully – whether in response to media interest or by taking the initiative – does not by itself resolve any specific negotiating difficulty. Media news and comment can, though, influence attitudes and thus have a potentially powerful effect on the resolve of those involved and on the degree of support or opposition that they experience from the public at large.

Key points

- Negotiations cannot be conducted through the media, but the media can be used to influence the attitudes of those concerned, as well as – where appropriate – public understanding and support.
- The common characteristics of media communications of all kinds are accuracy, clarity, and reasonableness.
- Press advertisements offer full control over what is said, but their status as advertisements may reduce their credibility.
- Press releases provide initial control over content, but it cannot be guaranteed that they will be reproduced fully, or at all.
- Press releases need to be written in the style of the media to which they are issued.
- Journalists may be assisted or persuaded to write news stories. These may carry more public credibility than company statements, but incur the risk of error or distortion.
- Radio or TV interviews should be seen as opportunities to put across a message in clear, simple terms, regardless of the precise questions asked.

17

Influencing Managerial Negotiations

In previous chapters, negotiation has been considered as an activity that occurs in many different contexts; examples have been drawn from formal and informal negotiations, and from managerial, commercial, and industrial relations settings. In this and the next two chapters, the specific characteristics of each of these three settings are examined in more detail. The question being dealt with is: what features of each setting influence the nature and success of negotiation in that context? In this chapter we look at the informal negotiating interactions between managers that are an integral element of the whole management process. The general factor is that managers have working relationships extending beyond the scope of any single issue. Their ability to influence one another in any specific negotiating episode will, therefore, be affected by the nature and quality of their general relationships. There are four major influences at work here:

- the relative status of the managers involved
- connections with sources of power in the organisation
- the creation of obligations
- the power of knowledge and expertise.

Status

Almost all organisations operate through management hierarchies, and the relative status of managers who are trying to influence one another has a marked effect on the outcome of their discussions.

Interaction between senior managers and their direct subordinates in the line cannot really be described as negotiation, because the seniors have ultimate authority to make decisions and override their subordinates' views. Power, in other words, is extremely one-sided. That is not to say that many negotiating skills cannot be used to good effect by a subordinate who is trying to persuade his or her line manager to adopt a particular line of action. But the ultimate right of the boss to make the final decision distinguishes this type of managerial interaction from real negotiation.

The situation is different when, say, two managers from different parts of an organisation meet for discussions – and this type of managerial contact occupies more of many managers' time than boss/subordinate meetings. Here, neither manager can exercise executive authority over the other. The outcome of discussions should depend on their skills of argument and persuasion. Where two managers' status is perceived as equal, this is very much the case. So when the chief accountant meets the chief buyer to suggest that a change to purchasing schedules would reduce the cost of stock holdings – and both managers are at the same hierarchical level – the outcome will depend largely on their respective negotiating ability.

Suppose, though, that a meeting of this kind takes place between two managers of different status. The chief accountant may, for example, have sent a section accountant (a lower managerial level) to talk to the chief buyer. In this case, the status difference may have an unspoken effect. The chief buyer may feel more confident to express opposition; the accountant may feel inhibited in pressing the case as strongly as the chief accountant would have done. There are some senior managers who exploit status differences quite crudely, but this type of status influence is often quite subtle. It may not even occur to the senior of the two that the other, and less senior, manager is being inhibited by having to deal with someone at a higher level in the hierarchy. The following example illustrates this:

A local authority chief executive set up a working party to plan the reorganisation and re-equipment of the central administrative offices. The members of the working party were drawn from the finance, office services, and personnel departments. The four members of the finance and office services departments were all 'third-tier' staff (two levels below the heads of the departments) and paid on a senior management grade. The single personnel department representative was a 'fifth-tier' training officer, on a much lower management grade.

The working party's final recommendations, though generally very sound, were found in practice to have underestimated the volume of office staff training required to operate the new word-processing equipment. The training officer on the working party was asked by his boss to explain why he had not ensured that training was given adequate attention. The training officer replied that he had recognised this weakness in the working party's deliberations before its recommendations were finalised. 'But', he went on, 'I became aware at around this time that I was the most junior member of the working party. I think this prevented me from arguing as forcibly as I should have done for more attention to be given to staff training.'

Two lessons arise from this example:

● For senior managers, the message is never to underestimate the effect of status differences on the confidence of junior staff, including those in departments other than their own. If a positive contribution is looked for from a junior manager, equally positive encouragement and support may need to be given to overcome the inhibiting influence of status.

● For junior managers, the message is to think through the issue positively and to realise that in managerial discussions outside the direct executive line, their ability to negotiate effectively stems from factors other than status – particularly from the expertise they can demonstrate in relation to the subject under discussion.

Connections with sources of power

Just as status can be used manipulatively by a senior to 'squash' a junior opponent, so the juniors may be able to use the existence of their connections with other useful powerful managers as a manipulative response. This is not a very attractive feature of managerial life: in an ideal world all managerial negotiations would be resolved as a result of a rational and impersonal analysis of the issues. But if an able young manager is faced with manipulative opposition, the use of connections may become necessary. The point can be illustrated by the case of a young woman manager who was being obstructed by a prejudiced and status-conscious older senior male manager:

Anne McTarg was the newly appointed personnel officer of a manufacturing company that had recently been taken over by a large conglomerate. The new chief executive, Bill Fraser, wanted to introduce a whole range of modern management techniques, with a particular emphasis on systematic performance appraisal. He had selected Anne for her job largely because of her previous work as a management trainer in which she had specialised in appraisal training. He had also told her – though this was not known by other managers – that she would have his whole-hearted backing in putting in an appraisal system, though he wanted this 'sold' to the managers, rather than imposed.

Anne succeeded in generating interest and support for a training programme as a precursor to the new system with all the managers but one: George Garnet, the crusty, 58-year-old production manager. At her meetings with him, he persisted in dealing with her ideas in a flippant manner, emphasised that as a member of the senior management team (which Anne was not) he knew what was needed better than she did, and generally indicated that he could not take the ideas of a young, junior and female manager seriously.

There came a stage at which all but Garnet's staff were scheduled for the training courses, while he still prevaricated about their involvement. Anne felt that she had no alternative but to use the support she knew she would get from Bill Fraser – but she wanted to avoid a direct appeal for his help. She took an opportunity one lunchtime of sharing a table with Fraser in the staff canteen. The following morning she made a point of running across Garnet in the factory. 'I was having lunch with Bill yesterday,' she said, 'and he was asking whether all departments had yet signed up for the appraisal training course. Can I expect your nominations this week?'

This set Garnet's alarm bells ringing. 'Bill', he noted, not 'Mr Fraser': perhaps this young woman carried more managerial clout than he had realised, and his training nominations were rapidly forthcoming.

This is, of course, a somewhat crude example of the power of connections. Normally, things do not have to be spelled out or hinted at so directly. A manager's connections with power sources become known and are then an unspoken influence on managerial negotiations. What they do is alter the power balance, and they are, therefore, of particular importance for the manager who is otherwise in a weak bargaining position. The danger is that they can be used to support weak arguments and may, therefore, result in poor decisions' being made. Furthermore, managers who use their informal contacts with power sources in an obviously manipulative manner generate much personal resentment. They may also be disowned by the seniors with whom they claim connections if they exploit such relationships too openly. That said, it is still advisable in many managerial negotiations to be aware of informal power groupings and connections. Who has links with whom? From whom might someone obtain support? Assessments of all aspects of relative strength are necessary if bargaining expectations are to be realistic.

Obligations

Negotiations between managers may be quite strongly influenced by the general quality of their working and personal relationships – a factor that distinguishes this form of negotiation from many commercial or legal transactions in which the interacting parties meet only in the context of the negotiations. If the general relationship between managers is friendly, constructive, and based on mutual respect for each other's expertise, then their negotiations will be equally soundly based. The outcomes will derive far more from a rational assessment of the issues than from considerations of status, connections, or point-scoring.

The converse is, unfortunately, also true: that if a working relationship is tainted by personal rivalry, any negotiating episode is likely to be treated as a conflict in which concern about winning or losing will take precedence over producing effective, agreed solutions.

Some managers, aware of the strong influence of personal factors, set out deliberately to create a sense of obligation among their colleagues. They will be very helpful on issues that are not of major concern to them in order to build up a stock of goodwill which they can call on when their turn comes to seek something from other managers. So a manager may offer to assist a colleague whose section is temporarily short-staffed not out of a genuinely collaborative attitude, but to create a sense of obligation to influence a later negotiating episode.

An ambitious, newly appointed chief fire officer in a local authority was developing plans to achieve more autonomy in staff management matters. For this, he knew he would have to over-come resistance from the personnel director. Keeping his plans under wraps at this stage, he set out to 'cultivate' the personnel director by all possible means.

In management team meetings, he gave the personnel director strong support on several issues (not affecting the fire service) when the latter's plans were being attacked by other senior managers. He also began inviting the personnel director and his wife to attend fire service social functions, offering to provide a fire service car and driver. Invitations for such functions had not been made by his predecessor.

Fortunately, the personnel director spotted this attempt to create obligations at a very early stage, and found reasons politely to decline any but the more genuine and work-related offers of support.

This example makes the point that the wise manager, while determined to establish constructive and friendly working relationships, is very wary of accepting unsolicited gifts (actual or metaphorical) however innocent such offers may seem. If a sense of obligation is a powerful influence on managerial bargaining, the only effective counter is to avoid obligations being created.

The power of expertise

The influence that stems from a manager's expertise on the matter under debate is a powerful and constructive counter to the negative, manipulative influences discussed earlier in this chapter. Young or more junior managers may find their negotiating positions on particular issues undermined by the wiles of older and more senior managers who have developed the skills of organisational politics. But in the longer term, managers – whatever their age or status – who can demonstrate a mastery of their subject and an ability to apply this to organisational issues will succeed in becoming influential in intermanagerial discussions and bargaining.

Not that the mere possession of knowledge and ideas is sufficient: the manager has to develop the ability to project these into the discussion in a way that makes an impact on the other participants. Partly, this involves acquiring a positive verbal style and the confidence, if it becomes necessary, to interrupt a discussion with a firm correction or interjection. Assertiveness training can help overcome an initial tendency to be overcautious about taking issue in a discussion.

Two other methods of gaining attention and providing a focus to a discussion are:

- to distribute a document or chart that either highlights the key points or provides supporting evidence. So in a discussion about measures to improve recruitment, in which differences of view exist about the costs of job advertising, a document showing an analysis of the response rates of different advertising media may focus the discussion on specific, rather than generalised, factors. It may also assist an otherwise unassertive manager to stress a case for which a purely verbal presentation has not yet made much impact.

- to use a flipchart to write up key points, or to chart the logic of the case being made. Obviously, a flipchart or wall board cannot be used so spontaneously as a document, but where such use can be arranged, the user can exercise considerable control over the whole structure of the meeting. An otherwise unassertive or nervous negotiator can also gain much confidence from speaking to a prepared brief, and ensuring that key points are registered by writing them up as the discussion proceeds.

There is one important point to watch when the strength of one's negotiating position is based almost wholly on the knowledge and expertise one can bring to the issue under discussion: this is to ensure that what one puts forward is *correct*. A cynical, though successful, manager once said that there are two conditions that should govern any claimed statement of fact (or statistic): either that, if someone checks, the statement will be found to be correct; or that no one can check it! Without going this far, it is evident that credibility and influence based on knowledge and expertise are wholly undermined by any mistake or incorrect claim made on the basis of such knowledge. So the message is: prepare the case, check and doublecheck the facts, and then display this know-how positively and confidently. That way, even the most junior of managers will gain respect and be able to influence the outcome of negotiations with more senior managers.

Key points

- Managerial negotiations are affected by the quality of managers' general working relationships.
- Junior managers may be inhibited by, and manipulative senior managers may exploit, differences of formal status between participants in managerial discussions.
- A participant's known or assumed personal contacts or connections with powerful individuals or groups may result in his or her negotiating position being given more credibility than would otherwise be the case.
- Manipulative managers attempt to create a sense of obligation – which wise managers resist – in order to influence later negotiations.
- The manipulative aspects of managerial negotiations can be countered by the powerful influence of knowledge and expertise relevant to the solution of issues under discussion, clearly presented.

18

Influencing Commercial Negotiations

There are two main characteristics of commercial negotiations which, although not unique to this type of bargaining, have a major influence on its general characteristics:

- Most transactions are concerned with buying and selling, whether of goods or services or with associated matters such as specifications or delivery. In many cases, the primary factor under negotiation is financial. In most cases, too, the outcome of the negotiation is a legally enforceable contract.

- In many cases, the sole or main reason for a relationship between the two (or more) parties to negotiation is the subject under negotiation. This contrasts with managerial and industrial relations bargaining, in which the two parties have a working relationship that extends in scope and time well beyond the narrow limits of any one negotiating episode.

These two characteristics give commercial negotiations a sharper focus than some other forms of bargaining. During negotiations, either party has the option of abandoning the situation and seeking a buyer or seller elsewhere – an option not open in managerial or trade union bargaining. There is a simplicity in the final deal – in essence, a yes to a price. To this is coupled a need for precision about the parties' mutual commitments (about quality and delivery, for instance) because these are contractual obligations which, if needs be, must stand the test of the courts.

There is a further point: the balance of power in a buying-selling relationship is often in favour of the buyer, whereas in managerial and industrial relations situations the distribution of power is usually much more difficult to assess. Of course, the advantage is sometimes with the seller when a buyer's requirements can be met from only once source. Generally, though, the seller starts with the built-in disadvantage of having to overcome the buyer's resistance, while knowing that the buyer can turn to alternative sources of supply. Training in the skills of selling has, consequently, attracted far more attention than the art of buying. There is an extensive literature on salesmanship but, on buying, the bibliography is all but non-existent.

Negotiation in the internal market

The concept of the internal market, in which functions within an organisation 'purchase' one another's services, has injected a commercial element into working relationships between managers who have previously been encouraged to think of one another as collaborative colleagues. Negotiation in this context is not commercial in the full, legal sense because internal 'contracts' – generally termed 'service-level agreements' – are not enforceable at law. The sanction of taking disputes to court or to external conciliation or arbitration does not exist. Nevertheless, there are powerful pressures on the two parties to reach a formal and fully documented agreement, and to demonstrate their ability to negotiate effectively by avoiding any resort to higher levels of management to obtain a resolution of any failure to agree. These pressures are particularly acute if the purchaser has the authority to use external sources as an alternative to the in-house provider.

Many managers – particularly in the public sector, where internal trading is now widespread – have found it difficult to adjust to this market approach, and their negotiating styles have tended to be at one or other ends of a bargaining spectrum. At one extreme, as noted earlier in this book, an aggressive and confrontational style is adopted. The purchaser (client) takes the line that the provider (contractor) is in a weaker and subservient position and must simply accept anything that the purchaser specifies. The contractor sees the new role as being to make as much money as possible from internal charging, and uses every trick in the book to achieve this – such as imposing punitive extra charges for variations to the original specification or even charging for work that has not been done. At the other extreme, managers who are uncomfortable about their new roles may avoid the clarification of matters on which they realise there may be different views – such as the definition of quality standards – and simply fudge their agreements for the sake of a quiet life.

Internal market negotiations are best conducted in the context of two influencing factors – one procedural, one attitudinal. The procedural element is to follow a systematic process in the production and documentation of the necessary agreement. CIPFA (the Chartered Institute of Public Finance and Accountancy) has produced a guide to service-level agreements, on which the following recommendations are based. It suggests producing two documents – one setting out the general principles, the other providing a detailed specification.[1] The general statement (equivalent to the body of a commercial contract) includes the following points:

- a general description of the service to be provided
- the two parties to the agreement
- the duration of the agreement
- charging arrangements
- a notice period
- arrangements for monitoring and review
- insurance liability
- penalties for non-performance
- a procedure for settling disputes
- the information and resources that the purchaser has to provide
- contact points for both parties.

The specification should include clear definitions of the following points:

- the precise nature of the services provided
- volumes and quality standards of these services
- what optional services may be available on request
- a procedure for variations
- response times.

Using these check-lists, a systematic approach to negotiation can begin by discussing and agreeing the broad framework before moving on to the detail. This avoids running into early difficulties because of disagreement on a single, and possibly quite narrow, issue such as a notice period for the termination of the agreement. When dealing with the details, it can also be helpful temporarily to set aside any particular issue on which agreement proves difficult, and move on to other points that are easier to resolve. The more controversial issue can then be addressed later, after agreement has been reached on most of the other issues. By that time, both parties should be feeling pleased with their joint ability to make progress and will be less willing for a single issue to prevent a final agreement than if disagreement had been allowed to dominate the earlier part of the negotiation.

The attitudinal factor that should influence internal market negotiations is the underlying recognition by both parties that they work for the same organisation and share responsibility for contributing to its survival and success. In 'real' commercial negotiations, neither purchaser nor supplier may have any strong reason to be concerned about the viability of the other organisation. The purchaser is probably able to go to an alternative source; the supplier can secure other clients. But the in-house purchaser and provider should have a common organisational concern, and this can have a significant influence on their negotiating style. The real test of the options they discuss is: 'What is in the best long-term interests of the organisation?', not 'What is best for the short-term interests of the purchaser or provider?'

Sales techniques

This book is not intended as a manual on sales negotiations, but a summary of the selling ploys suggested by much of the literature and sales training programmes illustrates the effort needed to overcome the seller's normal disadvantages:

- Avoid or reduce the direct effect of competition with other suppliers by projecting your product or service as unique. Emphasise the differences between your product and its competitors – not the similarities.
- Flatter the buyer as a person of wisdom and discretion who is able to perceive the advantages that your product has over its competitors.
- Stress how your product will improve the buyers' position in relation to their competitors, or will reduce their costs or improve their image.

- Make the buyers feel uneasy about not keeping up to date with new products and developments. Suggest that their competitors may steal a march on them by getting in first.
- Suggest that delay in placing an order may have the disadvantage of an impending price rise or delayed delivery – or that an immediate order will carry unusually favourable terms.

Put as simply as this, these may seem like the crude, doorstep practices of the double-glazing salesperson. Yet, in essence, ploys of this kind lie behind much of the bargaining of the apparently more sophisticated world of large-scale commercial negotiations.

General bargaining principles

A broader set of principles can also be distilled from the commercial literature, and a number of these points have an application beyond the world of business negotiation. In producing the following list, acknowledgements are due particularly to the books of Winkler[2] and Scott.[3]

- Do not negotiate if you can obtain your objectives some other way. Why get into a situation in which you may have to make concessions, or agree to compromise, if you have the ability to obtain what you want without bargaining?
- Do not enter into negotiations without very thorough research and planning. Be prepared – have all the necessary facts and figures at your disposal, and be clear about your objectives and upper and lower limits.
- Try to create a pleasant but business-like climate: do not be provoked into unpleasantness or aggression.
- Maintain the initiative. State your important major requirement firmly and at an early point, thus forcing the other party to take on the harder task of trying to obtain concessions.
- Reveal the strength of your position by degrees: seek agreement primarily by the logic of your case, rather than by threatening sanctions. Use raw power sparingly.
- Look for ways of giving the other party some sense of satisfaction or achievement – perhaps on aspects of only minor importance to you – so that they are conditioned to make

complementary moves towards your position. Trade concession for concession.

- Leave yourself room for manoeuvre, either by asking for more than you would ultimately be prepared to accept, or by including some peripheral elements in your claim that you are prepared to abandon if, in so doing, the main objective can be achieved.
- Retain your integrity. Although negotiation may involve tough talking and manoeuvre, never use false data to support an argument and, if you make a commitment or promise, keep it. Effective bargains are all but impossible to conclude if the two parties do not trust each other's statements or intentions.
- Try to listen more than talk. Ask questions more than make statements. The more you listen, the more you will learn about the other side's case, and the less they will learn about yours.
- Avoid an impasse by having alternative ideas or topics to switch to if confrontation or breakdown seems imminent.
- Allow time for the other party to come to terms with your stated objectives. Do not press too hard for agreement while they are adjusting to the nature or size of your opening bid.
- Clinch agreement at a favourable moment when the bargaining relationship is on a high, and do so briskly and positively, closing the door on renewed discussion.

Contractual implications

It has already been noted that most commercial negotiations result in an agreement that is contractually enforceable. The agreement itself may be in the form of a legal contract document, such as results from the negotiation of a building lease between landlord and tenant. But agreements can be backed by the force of contract law when there are no formal contract documents – only, say, an exchange of letters – or even when no documentation exists. An oral agreement by an office manager to an oral offer by a contractor to clean the office windows for a quoted sum can be enforced through the courts if either party claims the other is in breach – provided they can convince the court of the existence and terms of the agreement.

This emphasises, of course, the value of putting agreements in writing at the earliest possible date, and of the written agreement's being very specific and avoiding ambiguous or vague wording. Where goods and services are concerned, the detail is best set out in a detailed specification. The agreement, which may be by a formal exchange of correspondence, can then state that such and such a service or product will be provided 'in accordance with the attached and agreed specification'.

In the absence of clear documentation, questions sometimes arise as to whether or not a contract has been concluded. If the terms of a contract are unclear, a dispute may arise about its meaning. These problems are avoidable, but not all managers understand the essential features of contract law. Although the complexities that can arise through litigation occupy many legal volumes, the basic principles of contract are very simple – and very important. They are as follows:

- A contract is concluded by a process of offer by one party and acceptance by the other. The agreement must involve 'consideration' – normally, some form of payment.
- Unless specifically stated to the contrary, the contract is concluded at the time of acceptance, whether or not this is documented. If this immediate and binding obligation is to be avoided, then words such as 'subject to contract', or 'subject to written conformation' must be used.
- If either party fails to fulfil its side of the bargain, the other can pursue the matter in the civil courts.
- Two legal remedies are open – an injunction that orders the other party to perform its side of the bargain, or to desist from action that prevents the bargain being met: or compensation for losses sustained by the failure to perform.
- A dispute about the interpretation of the terms of the contract can also be taken to the courts for resolution. The courts adopt a commonsense approach to such disputes. They ask either what the parties intended or, if even this is not clear, what a reasonable person might conclude that the parties intended.
- Contracts will be held to be invalid at law if they include unlawful or illegal provisions, or if one party has led the other to conclude an agreement by deceitful or dishonest means.

All this supports the advice by experienced and effective

125

commercial negotiators that agreements should be in writing, specific in their terms, avoid ambiguity, and be concluded on the basis of an honest presentation of relevant information.

Key points

- Commercial negotiations often differ from other forms of bargaining in that the two parties have no working relationship outside the issues under negotiation.
- Internal market negotiations should focus on the joint responsibility of purchaser and provider for the survival and success of the organisation they both work for.
- The most common feature of commercial negotiations is buying and selling – often to produce a contractually binding agreement.
- In buying and selling, the balance of power frequently lies with the buyer who can choose to deal with an alternative source of supply.
- Consequently, business literature and training programmes concentrate far more on developing selling skills than on the expertise involved in buying.
- Sales techniques include the avoidance of direct competition by emphasising the unique qualities of the goods or services being sold, an emphasis on the benefits of a deal to the buyer, and encouraging the buyer to make an immediate decision.
- General bargaining principles include an emphasis on careful planning, the trading of concessions, and the avoidance of impasse.
- Because most commercial agreements constitute legally enforceable contracts, it is important that they should be in writing, unambiguous, and founded on a basis of accurate information.
- Legal remedies for breach of contract include injunctions to enforce performance and also compensation for financial damages.
- Contracts are legally invalid if they include unlawful or illegal provisions, or were obtained by dishonesty or deceit.

References

[1] WINKLER, J. *Bargaining for Results.* London, Heinemann, 1981.
[2] SCOTT, B. *The Skills of Negotiation.* Aldershot, Gower, 1987.
[3] *Service-Level Agreements.* London. CIPFA, 1991.

19

Influencing Negotiations with Trade Unions

Negotiations in an industrial relations context can vary from the informal discussion between an individual manager and a shop steward, to a major, national pay-bargaining session between the representatives of an employers' association and a confederation of trade unions. Despite these major differences of scale and style, there are several common features that influence the effectiveness of negotiations. These are:

- the quality of personal relationships between the two parties
- the existence of agreed negotiation and disputes procedures
- the importance of precedents
- the impact of trade union legislation.

Personal relationships

Managers (and shop stewards) who have an interest in the speedy resolution of actual or potential disputes should recognise the importance of establishing and cultivating a constructive working relationship with those with whom they may, from time to time, have to negotiate. Personal animosity or distrust creates a barrier to the effective, joint discussion of difficult issues and the evolution of jointly satisfactory compromise. The converse is also true: that if the participants in negotiation understand and respect one another as individuals, the negotiation is far more likely to succeed.

Skilled personnel managers are well aware of this, and work hard to establish a relationship with their opposite numbers on the trade union side which is akin to that of fellow professionals. The underlying attitude is: 'We may be on opposite sides of the table, but we both know the score so far as industrial relations are concerned, and we share an interest in conducting our affairs on a fair, business-like and intelligent basis.' Breakdowns in negotiation can reflect badly on the professional competence of the negotiators on either side. An example illustrates this cultivation of trust and confidence:

Judith Cliffe was the personnel manager of a company manufacturing components for the motor trade. George Winnall was the factory convenor of shop stewards. The company began to suffer from stock losses from the finished goods stores – probably through employee pilfering. Before taking any formal or overt action, Judith took George aside in the canteen one day and said: 'I don't know whether you've heard anything about this, George, but we may have to come to you formally soon to talk about action to stop stock losses. The security people suspect pilferage, and we may have to consider random searches. You might find it useful to do a bit of scouting around before the next weekly meeting with the stewards.'

A few weeks later (after the stock problem had been resolved without the need for any drastic tightening of security), George called in to Judith's office on an informal visit – she maintained an open-door policy for such approaches. After a few minutes of apparently general chat, George said: 'By the way, Fred the Red is up for election as toolroom steward next month. He stands a pretty good chance if the toolroom manager persists in his daft plan to publicise individual quality records.' George then went on to talk briefly about another topic and then left. At no time had he asked for anything specific.

For the personnel manager in this example to talk about the stock losses in advance of any formally determined action carried some risks. The convenor might have reacted strongly to the implication that some of his members were pilfering the stock, or even have done something to prejudice the company's investigations of the thefts. But the personnel manager and convenor trusted each other, and this informal contact reaffirmed the trust. Both also recognised, though this did not have to be articulated, that confidences from one party on one topic needed eventually to be reciprocated by the other on some other matter. In other words, what was being created was almost a trading relationship. This was evidenced by the convenor's later hint about the way the election of a confrontational shop steward might be avoided.

Procedures

Apart from very informal negotiations, the processing of most industrial relations issues is governed by formally agreed procedures. This is partly a matter of long-standing convention and partly a feature of industrial relations promoted by ACAS codes of practice. The main reason for having agreed procedures is to enable matters to be dealt with quickly, without the need for preliminary discussions about how and when the negotiations are to be arranged. One disadvantage is that a departure from the procedure, however minor, may become the cause of a subsidiary dispute – sticking to procedure having become an end in itself. There are five main elements in most procedure agreements:

- *Levels of negotiation:* which issues can be negotiated at which levels in the organisation's hierarchy. In a large company or local authority, for example, there are often three levels:
  - workplace, eg depot, office unit, workshop
  - divisional or departmental
  - company or council.
- *Participants:* who, on each side, takes part in negotiations at each level. For example:
  - at workplace level, the shop stewards with their immediate local managers
  - at divisional level, divisional union representatives with divisional managers and their personnel specialists
  - at company level, full-time union officials, the stewards' convenor, company directors and the group personnel manager.
- *Time-scales:* a definition of the time periods within which meetings must be arranged after an issue has first been notified by one party to another; and the time limits governing the progression of unresolved issues from one level to the next.
- *The conduct of meetings:* particularly, who will chair the negotiations. This may always be left to management, or may alternate between management and the trade unions, or may (in a few cases, mainly at national level) involve the joint appointment of an independent person such as an academic or lawyer.
- *Agenda and minutes:* how items are to be submitted for negotiation – whether or not a documented case is needed; the form

minutes are to take (brief notes on what has been agreed, and action points; or a full record of the discussion); and whether minutes are subject to agreement between joint secretaries or are left to management to produce.

In addition to the influence of formal procedure agreements in defining the structure and conduct of negotiations, collective bargaining is also influenced by the unwritten ritual of claim, offer, counter-claim, revised offer, and so on. There is an expectation that a union will eventually agree a lower figure (eg for a pay award) than they originally claimed; and a similar expectation that the employer will improve on the first offer. In that both parties are fully aware of these likely moves, they seem to cancel each other out. The routine of high claim, low offer seems necessary – less as a good method of reaching an agreed outcome than as a ritual that provides a degree of predictability in an otherwise uncertain situation. In recent years, this convention has been put under severe strain by employer or union refusing to move from their opening position. The resentment of the other party to such obduracy has sometimes appeared to be as much a reaction to a failure to play by the normal rules as it has to the substance of the issue under negotiation.

Precedents

Custom, practice, and precedent have a much greater influence on trade union negotiations than in the managerial or commercial fields. Previous agreements, or established practices, tend to be treated as binding (in honour, not at law) until they are superseded by new agreements. This has the advantage of ensuring a degree of stability in the relationships between the two parties. However, it can also create major difficulties if one party comes to consider an agreement or working practice to have become outdated, whereas the other party (often the trade union) takes the view that the agreement is satisfactory, and is, therefore, unwilling to renegotiate the issue.

One way of avoiding such an impasse is for formal agreements to have a designated termination or review date – a practice common in the USA but less used in the UK.

On a less formal basis, both managers and trade union officials tend to refer back to previous decisions, documented or not, as creating rights that can be used as a bargaining factor.

Thus, a dispute arose in a construction company when an employee was dismissed for taking scrap materials from the joinery works. The union's argument was based on established custom, not on the morality of what had occurred. Employees have been taking scrap for years, said the union official, and the management have turned a blind eye to the practice. The management attempted to counter this by producing records of two resignations of employees which, they said, had occurred only because the employees had been caught taking scrap and had resigned to 'jump the gun' on what would otherwise have been a dismissal.

In the resultant negotiations as much time was spent arguing about what had happened in the past as on the particular facts of the case that had caused the dispute.

The common trade union position is that if something has been done in a particular way in the past, then any change must be subject to negotiation. The management position is often that if evidence can be produced to show that the change is not wholly without precedent, then no negotiation is necessary. Arguments about these conflicting views are singularly unconstructive, particularly if they result in a secondary dispute about the existence of precedent, rather than solving the matter in hand. The effective manager will understand the influence of precedent, will recognise when the trade union has the power to block or limit management action, and in those circumstances will enter negotiations with a plea to concentrate on the issue under dispute and the future, not on post-mortems on previous decisions.

Trade union legislation

Since 1979, legislation has had a growing influence on the conduct of industrial disputes. The law has not affected the conduct of negotiations directly, nor has it made collective agreements legally binding. These agreements still lie outside the purview of the law of contract, except insofar as their provisions are incorporated into individual employees' contracts of employment.

What the trade union legislation has done is markedly to reduce the power of trade unions to take coercive action against employers, and to strengthen the ability of employers to use the law against such action. In short, the legislation has altered the balance of power in favour of employers. Two weapons have been made available to employers:

- *Injunctions:* these are orders of the court to desist from, or to take, specified action. They are very powerful instruments because to ignore them amounts to contempt of court, for which the courts have unlimited power to impose penalties – including imprisonment.
- *Damages:* these are orders to pay designated sums in compensation for financial losses.

In outline, the particular features of trade union legislation are these:

- It is not unfair to dismiss employees who are on strike, providing all are treated equally.
- Trade unions can be injuncted or sued for damages for taking industrial action if this action adversely affects an employer who is not directly involved (ie secondary action).
- Trade unions can also be injuncted or sued if they initiate industrial action without first conducting a ballot among the employees concerned. The law prescribes in considerable detail how such ballots are to be conducted, and unions can thus be sued for failing to meet these conditions.

The case-law surrounding the interpretation of trade union legislation is complex and still in a state of development. This book is not the place for the lengthy legal exposition needed to set out all the implications of this legislation. The subject is referred to here as a reminder to negotiators that legal rights and duties are a factor meriting close consideration when planning a negotiating strategy. Expert legal advice is essential before launching court action, but on a more informal basis, management negotiators may sometimes need to let the union negotiators see that they are aware of the limitations the law now imposes on industrial action. For example, a threat of immediate strike action by an inexperienced shop steward might be countered with a comment that: 'You do know that it is unlawful to start a strike without first holding a ballot?' Whether such a comment would improve or exacerbate the negotiating climate is, of course, a matter for judgement – but there may still be some lay union officials who do not fully understand the extent to which coercive action has been circumscribed.

Key points

- The effectiveness of negotiations with trade unions is affected by the general quality of working relationships between managers and trade union officials.
- Effective management negotiators cultivate a positive relationship of mutual trust and respect with their trade union opposite numbers.
- The processes of formal negotiations are normally the subject of agreed procedures.
- These procedures determine the various levels of negotiation within the organisation's hierarchy, who the participants are, time-scales, the conduct of meetings, and the form of documentation.
- Industrial relations are strongly influenced by custom, practice, and precedent. General disputes about precedents can become as significant as the issues surrounding specific cases.
- Trade union legislation has severely limited the ability of trade unions to take coercive action and has therefore altered the balance of power in favour of employers.
- This legislation may need to be taken into account when evolving negotiating strategies; and some union officials may need to be reminded of its existence.

133

20

Negotiating Skills

As in most human activities, some people are inherently better at negotiating than others, but to describe the personality characteristics of the effective negotiator is little assistance to people who do not share those characteristics. Personalities cannot be changed. However, that is not to say that negotiating skills cannot be acquired or improved. With preparation and training, most managers can improve their skills in this important aspect of managerial activity. There are three broad factors involved, each with several elements:

- *knowledge:* of negotiating principles
  of the context of the particular negotiation
  of the detailed subject matter involved

- *skill:* in analysing the issues
  in personal interactions
  in communicating

- *attitudes:* towards the negotiating process
  towards the specifics of each negotiation
  towards one's own role.

Knowledge

No manager can feel confident and at ease in a negotiation without a broad understanding of the general context in which the negotiation occurs. As earlier chapters of this book have pointed out, the managerial, commercial, and industrial relations worlds all have their particular characteristics and conventions. A manager who does not understand the contractual implications of commercial bargaining, or who fails to appreciate the importance given by trade unions to the existence of precedents, runs the risk of major errors in bargaining tactics, however good he or she is as a 'natural' negotiator.

There are three areas of knowledge to consider:

- *Negotiating principles characteristic of the particular context.* In industrial relations, for example, it needs to be recognised that a trade union derives power and authority from its members – not from its paid union officials. Power in trade unions is derived from the bottom up – the opposite of the company system, in which power flows from the top down. Failing to understand this can result in great frustration for the manager who expects the union general secretary to exercise executive authority – when, in fact, this apparently powerful union leader has to refer negotiating concessions back to a committee or even has to ballot the whole membership.

  Similar misunderstandings can occur between managers who fail to appreciate the conventions of decision-making within the firm, or commercial negotiators who do not understand the technical, legal, or organisational constraints involved in the type of transaction concerned.

- *The context of the particular negotiation.* Effective negotiators understand the culture, conventions, constraints, and opportunities surrounding each negotiating episode. They also ensure that they are fully briefed about every surrounding feature that may affect the particular issues under discussion.)Who are the personalities on the other side? What are their negotiating strengths and weaknesses? What issues apart from those under direct discussion are of interest or concern, and which might influence the way the bargaining proceeds? What sequence of events triggered the situation that led to the need to negotiate? Will the stance that any of the negotiators takes be influenced by considerations of status, friendship, rivalry, animosity, or ambition?

- *The detailed subject matter of the negotiation itself.* The effective negotiator has a mastery of the subject under discussion, knowing that an ability to display an in-depth knowledge of the issues contributes powerfully to bargaining credibility. To go into negotiations without this depth and accuracy of information is extremely risky, and will probably be exploited by a skilled opponent.

A managing director met a trade union delegation, without preparation, to discuss their claim for two extra days' holiday at
Christmas. 'If it was a matter just for this firm,' he said, 'I would
be sympathetic; but as you know, we have always kept to
national agreements and I can't depart from that now.' The trade
union leader responded: 'You seem to be overlooking an adden-
dum to last year's national agreement which made it clear that the
annual leave provisions are distinct from any supplementary
leave companies may grant at bank holidays: so you haven't a
problem, and we'll accept your offer of two extra days at
Christmas!'

Part of the planning process for a negotiation is, therefore, to list
all relevant information and ensure that this is obtained (and is accurate and up-to-date) before negotiation begins.

Skill

Although certain aspects of negotiating ability may come more
naturally to some people than others, skill can be acquired or improved by training and practice. Three types of skill are particularly important:

- *analytical skills.* Some negotiations may involve consideration
  of a very complex interaction of various aims and concessions.
  An effective negotiating plan should therefore look analytically
  at the situation and consider such questions as:
  - What is the central issue? What are the peripheral issues?
  - What is the central objective? What are the subsidiary aims,
    and to what extent can these be traded for the main objec-
    tive?
  - What are the main barriers to achieving what we want?
  - What are the outside limits of an acceptable agreement?
  - What are the best tactics to achieve our main aim? How can
    we make the most effective use of sanctions and con-
    cessions?
  - What alternative approaches are there? What are their
    strengths and weaknesses?
  - Where are we most vulnerable? How can we best protect
    ourselves?

- What information do we need to support our case? And what to undermine the other party's position?
- What are the arguments and information most likely to be used by the other party?
- What contingency plans are needed should we fail to reach an acceptable agreement?

● *interactive skills.* This is the main area in which some people have natural talent but in which all can improve with positive effort, practice, and training. Good negotiators develop an ability to sense and influence the changing moods and concerns of individuals and groups, and encourage progress towards consensus. Much of this skill stems from particular ways of behaving, and although training in these skills is very much a matter of practice and coaching – rather than just reading about them – there are some behavioural traits worth remembering!

- A negative habit is to over-personalise issues by an inappropriate or too frequent use of the words 'I' and 'you'. Thus a manager may say: 'I cannot afford to go beyond 6 per cent', or 'It's not my policy to offer discounts for prompt payment.' This habit can be intensely irritating when the other party knows that the limits being described derive from team or corporate decisions or policy, and not from the personal authority of the speaker. Similarly, to respond to a proposal by the other party with 'I do not understand how you can justify that claim' is unnecessarily personal and provocative. A more impersonal and tactful response would be: 'That is a new point that needs more explanation.'

   The effective negotiator concentrates on the *issues*, not on the personalities.
- The temptation to score debating points can be very strong – but is usually best resisted. It can be very satisfying to spot a flaw in the other side's logic and to point this out in a somewhat gloating fashion. It is often better, though, to raise the point by asking a question that allows the other party to correct their mistake without loss of face. Thus: 'We don't quite follow the logic of that point. Could you explain in a bit more detail?' – rather than 'Do you realise that you have just contradicted yourself!'
- It is also tempting to spend time trying to allocate fault or blame. So a negotiation about new safety measures may

137

become bogged down in arguments about who was to blame for a recent accident. Generally, the better course in this type of situation is to say: 'Don't let's spend too much time on the past. We agree that improvements are needed. Let's concentrate on what now needs to be done to make things better in future.'

– A very important skill to develop is that of listening and questioning, rather than interrupting other speakers with counter-arguments, or making lengthy statements. There is no great mystique about acquiring this skill – it is very much a matter of being aware of its value and exercising self-discipline.

– A skill in which training is more likely to be required is the recognition of 'signals' – verbal or non-verbal – that indicate changes of thought or mood among the participants. There is a considerable literature on body language, and many clues as to how a negotiation is progressing can be picked up by observing changes in posture and gesture.

Allied to these skills of observation are those of use. For example, a point can be given emphasis by tapping one's papers; and attention can be gained and held by leaning forward and making direct eye contact with the other party.

– It is conducive to constructive discussion to end statements or comments on a positive, rather than negative, note. Thus, instead of saying: 'We are ready to consider your revised proposals about delivery schedules, but the bulk discount is still unacceptable', reverse the statement and say: 'The bulk discount is still a problem, but we are ready to consider your revised delivery proposals.' A negative end to a statement is likely to generate a negative response – and the reverse is also true.

● *communicating skills*. The ability to communicate effectively is part of the wider range of interactive skills just outlined. But negotiation involves written communication and documentation as well as face-to-face discussion, and clarity of exposition merits emphasis. There are two common failings: the use of unnecessarily formal or stilted language, and a tendency to be too indirect in relaying bad news.

A shop stewards' committee will not be impressed by a statement that: 'The company will have difficulty meeting your aspirations for this year's pay award owing to the past six months of negative growth in sales volumes and operating margins.' Better to tailor the language to the audience, and not wrap up an unpleasant message in jargon, by saying: 'We cannot afford the pay increase you have asked for because sales and profits have fallen.'

Attitudes

All behaviour is influenced by attitudes. However skilful a negotiator may be, the application of this skill is affected by the person's underlying attitude to the negotiating process, the particular features of the matter under discussion, or his or her own role and motivation.

● Some managers have an underlying resentment about the need, in some circumstances, to negotiate. It is an attitude that makes a particular impact in the field of industrial relations. A manager's perception of the role of the employer may be basically authoritarian – that employees should have undivided loyalty to their employer, and be ready to do what managers tell them. If this attitude is strongly felt, it will be difficult for the manager to accept that employees collectively (through their trade union) can challenge management's ability to manage, and that they have a right – or have acquired the power – to negotiate. Any managerial concession will be thought of as weakness rather than as constructive compromise.
● There may also be specific features of the negotiation in hand that influence how the participants behave. A manager will become defensive about a feature towards which he or she feels a sense of ownership – for example, a procedure or piece of equipment that the manager designed or selected. Changes may then be resisted not on the merits of the argument but on the basis of personal pride. Strong personal animosities (or friendships) between individual participants may also influence how they interact.
● Managers may have their own needs for recognition or achievement – a perception of themselves as good debaters, or wheeler-dealers, or persons of importance. A negotiation can

139

become an arena for the demonstration or realisation of these roles, rather than as a collaborative process to achieve an outcome that satisfies both parties. It is significant that when Lord Goodman (an outstandingly successful legal negotiator) was asked what the most important aspect of negotiation was, he replied with an attitudinal point – 'the determination to reach agreement.'

Problem cases

All the skills discussed in this chapter are needed from time to time when the manager has to deal with problem cases – negotiators who are either inexperienced and lack competence, or who have developed a particularly strong style that, they have discovered, is very effective in influencing and persuading others. They can be categorised as indecisive, emotional, confused, aggressive, or manipulative.

The indecisive negotiator

One of the most frustrating of problem cases is the negotiator who is very ready to discuss all the detail of the matter under consideration and options for an agreement, but lacks the confidence to make the formal, final decision. He or she sees difficulties where none exists, looks for reasons why every proposal will not work, asks for guarantees of success, and generally delays the arrival of the point at which a firm yes or no is needed.

Patience and reassurance are needed in dealing with the indecisive negotiator. Attempts to speed up the discussion or brush aside peripheral concerns only result in even more doubts and delays. Each objection should be addressed seriously and a careful step-by-step approach adopted, so that the final decision is little more than a confirmation of a series of points that have emerged in the course of the discussion. It may not be possible to give guarantees about the outcome, but a promise to review matters after a period, or a clause allowing the negotiations to be reopened in the event of some unexpected occurrence, may help to provide the reassurance that this type of negotiator needs.

Offering an adjournment so that the person can seek advice from a colleague can be another useful move.

The emotional negotiator

Emotional negotiators personalise the whole process and require very careful handling. They tend to see any objection to their point of view as personal criticism and react accordingly. Their response to what is intended as impersonal questioning of the logic or practicability of their arguments may well be a personal attack – alleging rudeness or ignorance rather than responding factually. Conversely, when they feel things are going well they may become overoptimistic and impatient, failing to raise points that should be considered if a sound agreement is to be achieved. A very careful choice of words is most important when dealing with the emotional negotiator. For example, the response to an unclear statement made by this type of negotiator should be something like: 'It might be helpful if that point could be more fully explained', not: 'You have not explained that point clearly enough.' Impersonal language and the avoidance of words or phrases that might be interpreted as being personally critical are what is needed. Outbursts of indignation should be allowed to burn themselves out: interrupting the emotional negotiator who is in full flow is likely to make matters worse. The temptation to make comments about their tendency to become emotional (such as 'I hope you feel better for getting that off your chest') should also be avoided. Accept the person for what he or she is; let him or her blow off steam if necessary, and then quietly return to the subject of the negotiation.

The confused negotiator

Confused negotiators find it difficult to follow complicated arguments or a logical sequence of discussion. Halfway through discussion on one point they think of something else and try to move the negotiation on to whatever comes immediately to mind. They may also fail to see the connection between different parts of the negotiation, and tend to want points settled that, in fact, should be deferred pending agreement on prior, related matters.

141

Negotiating to a phased agenda is one way of responding to the confused negotiator. For example, in a discussion that has to arrive at a plan to cut costs, insist on first identifying and agreeing the general area of cuts (eg office overheads), then move on to the particular items to target (equipment leasing charges), then to the precise action to take. If the confused negotiator raises a point in advance of the agenda, make a note of it and say it will be dealt with later. The use of flowcharts or other forms of visual presentation of data or concepts may also be useful in keeping negotiations on track.

The aggressive negotiator

The aggressive tactics used by some negotiators can seem much the same as the outbursts and personalised comments made by the emotional negotiator. However, there is a major and important difference: emotional negotiators are inherently defensive – their attacks are their way of preserving their own self-confidence or esteem, and they are more concerned with their own feelings than those of the other party. Aggressive negotiators, on the other hand, usually adopt aggressive tactics with the positive intention of throwing the other party off balance. Aggression is used as a weapon to achieve a result, whereas emotion is a largely uncontrolled personal reaction.

Aggression works only if it is allowed to. If an objective of the negotiation becomes the avoidance of unpleasantness, if things are conceded because of the vigour with which they have been argued, if points that needed discussion are not raised for fear of the reaction, then the aggressive negotiator will have won. In addition to a determination not to allow aggression to succeed, there are two main behavioural options:

● to terminate, calmly but firmly, the negotiation, saying it is not possible to continue until the discussion can proceed on a more constructive and courteous basis
● to keep any emotional reaction under control, ignore the aggressive provocation, concentrate on the issue under discussion, and continue to negotiate on the facts and merits of the case.

Aggression is a form of bullying, and the aggressive negotiator's initial bluster or attempt to establish psychological dominance can often be punctured by a firm refusal either to be provoked into a similar response, or to be bullied into submission.

The manipulative negotiator

One problem of dealing with the manipulative negotiator is recognising the manipulation! This type of negotiator will have thought about the psychology of the situation and the personal style and strong and weak points of the participants. He or she adapts style and tactics accordingly and uses whatever blend of logic, influence, charm, or aggression that he or she thinks is most effective. Particular points to watch for include:

- flattery – comments about how clever, perceptive, or important the other person is should be treated with caution. They may be genuine expressions of respect, but may also be indications of a manipulative approach.
- a markedly different tone adopted by a negotiator in a team situation when he or she is speaking to different members of the other party's team. This may simply indicate a high degree of sensitivity in interpersonal relations, but may equally be evidence of an attempt to drive a wedge between members of the team.
- subtle references to influencing factors, such as the negotiator's friendship with a senior manager.
- the use of appeals to good sense, or hints that to agree to certain proposals may have benefits beyond the substance of the negotiation – 'You scratch my back today and I'll scratch yours tomorrow.'

There is a fine line between the effective and the manipulative negotiator so far as tactics are concerned, but the distinguishing feature is the negotiator's real objective. The manipulative negotiator is out to win (largely for the sake of winning) and is concerned with gaining personal satisfaction from the way the outcome has been achieved. The effective negotiator is out to achieve an agreement that meets the needs of the situation that gave rise to the negotiation, and gains satisfaction from the contribution the outcome makes to organisational performance.

Developing the skills needed to handle different negotiating situations and different types of negotiator should feature in most personnel professionals' personal development plans. As the IPD's guide to CPD (Continuing Professional Development)[1] points out, there are many ways in which skills can be acquired and improved – development is not wholly dependent on attending formal training courses, useful though these may be. Among the ways in which negotiating skills can be developed are:

- through reading books such as this to learn about the principles, strategies, and tactics of effective negotiation
- studying the nature and outcomes of major publicised negotiations – such as some of the high-profile episodes in the UK's relationships within the EU
- role-playing a case-study in negotiation, or participating in a management game with a strong negotiating element – normally in the context of a formal training event
- sitting in on a negotiation as an observer, tracking the effectiveness of each party's style and strategy, and discussing this with the participants after the event
- seeking advice and ideas from a mentor
- holding a de-brief with colleagues in a negotiating team after each session to discuss progress and tactics
- seeking feedback about personal negotiating effectiveness from managers, colleagues, and support staff in the context of 360-degree appraisal
- self-analysis – conducting an honest appraisal of one's own negotiating performance after each episode, and noting successes and mistakes.

Key points

- Although some people are better natural negotiators than others, negotiating skills can be acquired or improved by practice, coaching and training.
- There are three main elements involved in improving one's negotiating abilities – knowledge, skills and attitudes.
- Effective negotiation demands a knowledge of the principles of the negotiating process, the context of the particular negotiation, and its detailed subject matter.
- The main types of skill involved are analytical, interactive and communicative.
- Different approaches are needed to deal effectively with different types of difficult negotiations.
- Negotiations are strongly influenced by underlying attitudes to the process itself, to the issues and personalities involved in the particular case, and by one's own self-perception and personal needs for recognition and achievement.
- Planning to improve one's negotiating skills should be an element in most personnel professionals' personal development plans.

Reference

[1] 'Continuing Professional Development: The IPD Policy', IPD, 1996

Index